Contents

Introduction

L ife after retirement can be one of your happiest and most fulfilling times—the final segment of a well-lived life—and now is no time to stop living your best life! Maybe you have a whole bucket list of ideas for your newfound freedom from the workplace.

Bucket lists can be simple and achievable but are not necessarily a big worldwide trip d. They could be just a roadmap for the next 20+ years of your life. If you had been able to semi-retire and ease your way into it after a lifetime of work, it might have been a bit easier. I know many of us, myself included, had much of our self-concept wrapped up in who we were regarding our careers. So, if you feel you are standing at the edge of a vast, unexplored landscape and are thinking, "What now?" then hold on because we will show you what to do with all your free time. Keep in mind that free time can be a tricky thing. Without a plan, it can quickly turn into endless hours of daytime TV and too many trips to the fridge.

That's where this book comes in. *The Happy Retirement Bucket List*

Handbook aims to help you manage this next phase of your life. It's filled with ideas to keep you active, engaged, and—most importantly—happy. Whether single, married, widowed, or somewhere in between, there's something here for you.

This book caters to those who are retired or considering retirement, full of life, and eager to savor every moment. It's for curious minds who love to learn, the health-conscious who want to stay fit, and social butterflies who cherish time with family and friends. Whether you're a gardener, a photographer, a crafter, or someone looking for a new passion, this book has you covered.

We'll dive into various topics, from personal growth and health to budget-friendly travel and creative hobbies. You'll find tips for volunteering, starting a side hustle, and even mastering the latest technology. We'll also explore ways to stay socially active, find local activities, and relax. Lifelong learning and managing finances are also on the agenda. Each idea comes with practical steps you can take to make it a reality.

The book is organized into clear, easy-to-follow chapters. Each chapter focuses on a different theme, for example, health, travel, or hobbies. You can read it from cover to cover or jump to the sections that interest you the most. Either way, you'll find plenty of actionable steps and resources to help you. All resources appear in **bold** text the first time they appear for easy reference.

I've done my homework to ensure that all the information in this book is current and accurate. You'll find data from reputable sources with tried-and-true tips. This isn't just a bunch of theories; it's practical advice you can use, and even though it's more than just a bucket list book, here is a list of popular bucket list ideas based on shared interests, goals, and experiences that align with this stage of life:

1. **Travel to Dream Destinations**—Whether visiting Europe, seeing the Northern Lights, going on a safari, or taking a road trip

across the U.S., travel is often a top priority.

2. **Learn a New Skill or Hobby**—Many want to learn a new language, take up painting, photography, cooking classes, or even play a musical instrument.

3. **Reconnect with Nature**—Many people in their 60s wish to hike a famous trail, camp under the stars, visit national parks, or spend more time outdoors.

4. **Complete a Fitness Goal**—Popular goals include running a marathon, participating in a triathlon, mastering yoga, or maintaining regular physical activity.

5. **Volunteer or Give Back**—Volunteering for a cause, mentoring others, or participating in community service projects can be fulfilling items on a bucket list.

6. **Spend Quality Time with Family**—Many people desire to spend time with grandchildren, host family reunions, or create lasting memories with loved ones.

7. **Explore Ancestry and Family History**—Many research their family tree, visit ancestral homelands, or document family stories and histories.

8. **Write a Book or Memoir**—Sharing life experiences, writing a memoir, or even exploring fiction writing can be common creative goals.

9. **Attend a Special Event**—Whether it's a concert by a favorite band, a major sporting event, or a festival like Mardi Gras or Oktoberfest, attending a dream event can be exciting.

These ideas reflect a blend of adventure, self-growth, and making meaningful connections. We will delve into some of these in-depth—and many other daily things you can consider for your best retirement.

So, are you ready to create the life you love during your retirement? Let's get started. This book is your roadmap to a fulfilling, active, and happy retirement. Dive in, explore the possibilities, and make the most of this exciting new chapter in your life.

Chapter One

Building Your Social Circle

A few years ago, my neighbor, Frank, retired from his job as an accountant. He was thrilled for the first few weeks—no more early morning alarms and rush-hour traffic. Soon, however, Frank felt a bit isolated. He missed the camaraderie of the office, the casual chats over coffee, and even the office gossip. One day, his wife suggested he join the local gardening club. Frank, who had never planted anything more than a few tomatoes, reluctantly agreed. Fast forward one year. Frank's garden is the envy of the neighborhood, and he's made more friends than he ever had at work. His social calendar is now filled with garden tours, plant swaps, and even garden-themed potlucks.

Building a social circle after retirement is vital for staying active. Research has shown that being part of multiple social groups positively impacts retirees' health and well-being. Social groups help combat loneliness and give you a sense of belonging. Whether you're into knitting, reading, or birdwatching, there's a club for you. Let's explore how to find and join local clubs and organizations to enrich your retirement.

This is the first chapter because it is the most important thing you can do in retirement—and before. Social isolation in retirement can have significant physical, emotional, and mental health effects. As people retire, they may lose regular social interactions at work, leading to increased feelings of loneliness or isolation. Here are some of the impacts of social isolation in retirement:

Mental Health Decline: Without regular social contact, retirees may feel disconnected, leading to feelings of sadness, loneliness, and anxiety. These feelings can intensify if there's a lack of purpose after retirement. Better cognitive functioning is linked to social engagement.

Physical Health Consequences: Social isolation leads to increased blood pressure, cholesterol levels, and risk of heart disease. Loneliness and lack of social interaction can negatively impact the immune system, making retirees more susceptible to illness. Research has shown a higher risk of early death, sometimes equated with other health risks like smoking and obesity.

Decline in Physical Activity: Socially isolated retirees are likelier to lead a sedentary lifestyle, further impacting health. Lack of exercise can exacerbate chronic conditions, such as diabetes, arthritis, and heart disease.

Reduced Quality of Life: Work often provides a sense of purpose, and meaningful social interactions or engagement in new activities are necessary for retirees to feel a sense of identity and purpose. Engaging with others contributes to overall happiness. Retirees may experience reduced life satisfaction without regular social interaction, making retirement less fulfilling.

Increased Dependency: Retirees who experience social isolation may become more dependent on a small group of people (such as family members or caregivers) for social and emotional support.

1.1 Joining Local Clubs and Organizations

Let's combat isolation by joining a club. These groups serve as social hubs to meet like-minded people, share your interests, and feel part of a community. Senior centers often offer daily activities ranging from bingo nights to fitness classes. These centers are fantastic places to start. They provide an environment where you can meet people and try new activities.

Hobby-based clubs are another excellent option. If you love gardening, playing cards, or sewing, you'll find a group of people who share your passion. These clubs often meet regularly, allowing you to build lasting friendships.

Cultural organizations, like heritage societies or language clubs, offer another avenue. They provide opportunities to celebrate your cultural background or learn about new ones. These groups often host events, lectures, and social gatherings that can enrich your life.

Finding these clubs and organizations is easy. Start by checking local newspapers and community boards. Libraries and community centers, like local park offices, often have information about local groups. They usually have lists of clubs and can point you in the right direction.

Websites like **Meetup.com** are where you can search for your interests and find groups nearby. Contact your closest community college, as they often have resources. Once you find a club that interests you, join it! You never know—you might end up like Frank, with a garden full of flowers and a heart full of new friendships.

Attend regularly to get the most out of these groups. Consistent participation helps you build trust and rapport with other members. Over time, you may take on leadership roles, which can deepen your involvement and give you a greater sense of purpose. Establishing a routine around these activities can also structure your days, making your retirement more fulfilling.

Of course, joining a new group can be intimidating. If you are shy or have social anxiety, do your best to step out of your comfort zone. Remember, everyone in these groups was new once. Start by attending a few meetings as a guest to get a feel for the group. Bring a friend along if it makes you more comfortable. Virtual club meetings are also an excellent option if getting out is difficult. Many groups now offer online meetings, allowing you to participate from the comfort of your home.

Mobility issues or lack of transportation might be a barrier. Look for clubs that offer virtual options or consider carpooling with other members. Don't let these challenges stop you from enjoying the benefits of joining a club. As a retiree, I often use UBER; check out **gogograndparent.com,** which offers an UBER-like option for seniors.

Joining local clubs and organizations can transform your retirement. So, take that first step. Check out local bulletins, search online, and contact community centers. Find a club that interests you, then dive in.

1.2 Hosting and Attending Social Gatherings

Social gatherings are the lifeblood of any community, and retirement is the perfect time to enjoy them. To make it easy, schedule a potluck, where everyone brings their favorite dish. You may discover that your neighbor makes the best lasagna you've ever tasted. These small gatherings can create bonds that last a lifetime.

Themed gatherings, too, can add a sprinkle of excitement to your social calendar. A fun time could be a game night with stakes as high as the rent of a Monopoly hotel on Park Place or a movie night under the stars, complete with popcorn and classic films. The seasonal celebrations and holiday events give you the perfect excuse to dust off those festive decorations and bring people together for a good time.

Hosting a successful gathering starts with some planning, but don't worry—it's more manageable than it sounds. Begin by creating a guest list. Consider who you'd like to invite; mix old friends with new acquaintances to keep things lively. Once you have your list, send out invites. Depending on your style, these can be as simple as a quick phone call or as fancy as mailed invitations. Keep the food and drinks simple. Including a mix of appetizers, finger foods, and a couple of main dishes does the trick—this way, you can accommodate individual preferences and dietary restrictions. Arrange seating to encourage conversation and a warm, inviting atmosphere.

Icebreaker games are excellent tools for starting conversations. Fun activities like charades or a trivia quiz can help everyone relax and get to know each other. Look for events that align with your interests. If you love gardening, attend a plant swap; if you're a bookworm, attend a literary festival. Aligning your interests with the event's theme ensures you'll find like-minded people and feel more comfortable.

If you aren't up for entertaining at home, try new restaurants. Local fairs and festivals allow you to enjoy music, food, and crafts while mingling with your neighbors. Charity events and fundraisers provide social interaction and give you a sense of contributing to a more significant cause. Neighborhood block parties or picnics are fantastic for meeting new people and strengthening community ties. These social settings can be less intimidating because they're casual, and everyone is there to have a good time. Stepping outside of your comfort zone requires bravery. The great thing is that once you tap into that courage, it can grow stronger and affect other areas of your life. It's like unlocking a hidden strength that pushes you toward unexpected and rewarding experiences.

Trying new things offers many benefits to seniors, such as keeping their brains sharp and active, expanding their social activities to make new friends, and bringing variety, which can give their lives a sense of vibrancy and engagement.

1.3 Volunteering in Your Community

Volunteering is like a secret weapon that keeps you busy and enriches your life in ways you might not expect. When you volunteer, you're not just filling time; you're making new friends with similar values, contributing to causes that matter, and picking up new skills. It might be a lot of fun helping out at an animal shelter, where you get to cuddle with adorable pets and meet fellow animal lovers. Or think about assisting at a food bank, where your efforts directly impact those in need and forge bonds with other kind-hearted volunteers.

The best part is that there's a volunteer opportunity for everyone, no matter your interests or abilities. If you're more into books and learning, schools and libraries often seek volunteers to help with reading programs or organize community events. Environmental enthusiasts can enjoy taking part in clean-up efforts, planting trees, or maintaining community gardens. If you have spent your career in the business field, check out

SCORE.org, an organization that offers the opportunity to help younger business owners with much-needed advice.

Getting started with volunteering is easier than you think. Volunteer matching websites like **VolunteerMatch** or **Idealist** are fantastic resources. You can search by your interests, location, and availability to find the perfect fit. Local non-profits and community centers are also great places to start. They often have volunteer coordinators who can discover opportunities that use your skills and interests. Remember never to underestimate the power of networking, too. Talk to friends and family about their volunteer experiences. They might introduce you to a cause that resonates with you.

Many organizations offer flexible hours. You can volunteer as much or as little as you like, fitting it around your schedule. Physical limitations pose a challenge, but many roles don't require strenuous activity. For example, you might help with administrative tasks, phone calls, or virtual volunteering opportunities you can do from home.

Whether you spend an hour a week mentoring a young person or dedicating a Saturday to cleaning up a park, your efforts make a difference. Plus, the social connections you form and the sense of purpose you gain are invaluable. So, go ahead and take that first step. Contact a local non-profit, sign up on a volunteer-matching site, or simply ask around. You'll find that volunteering not only fills your time but also fills your heart.

1.4 Using Social Media to Stay Connected

Imagine your grandchild's face lighting up when they see your comment on their latest photo or your old high school buddy reaching out because they saw your post about a recent trip. Social media isn't just for the younger crowd; it's a powerful tool for connecting and making new friends at any age. Platforms like **Facebook** and **Instagram** offer endless opportunities to engage with others. Joining Facebook groups related to your interests—gardening, vintage car collecting, or knitting—can connect you with people who share your passions. Local community pages provide updates on events and activities, keeping you in the loop about what's happening nearby. Instagram is an excellent way to share your hobbies and connect with like-minded individuals through photos and hashtags. It's like having a giant scrapbook everyone can admire and comment on.

You are likely already on a social media platform. You can control who sees your posts and personal information. It's like having a lock on your virtual front door. Adjust these settings to a level you're comfortable with. Safety first, right? Beyond Facebook, platforms like Instagram and **LinkedIn** offer unique ways to connect. Instagram is great for visual storytelling, and LinkedIn is great for professional networking. Each platform has its charm, so explore and see which one suits you best.

Social media isn't just about staying in touch; it's a goldmine for learning and entertainment. You can access online tutorials and workshops on virtually any topic—cooking, photography, even how to play the ukulele. Virtual book clubs and discussion groups are another fantastic opportunity. They allow you to discuss your latest read with people from all over the world. And let's not forget the endless stream of inspirational content. Whether motivational quotes, heartwarming stories, or stunning travel photos, there's always something to brighten your day.

So, there you have it. Social media can be a fantastic way to stay connected, learn new things, and entertain yourself. The possibilities are endless, whether you're commenting on a grandchild's post, joining a virtual book club, or sharing your latest hobby project on Instagram. It's all about finding what works for you and diving in.

1.5 Participating in Group Activities and Classes

Participating in group activities and classes can be a delightful way to enrich your retirement life. I can't think of a better way to start your day than with a gentle yoga class, where you stretch and breathe in unison with a group of friendly faces. These classes improve your physical health and provide a structured setting for social interaction.

Exercise classes like yoga or aerobics are fantastic for maintaining fitness while enjoying the camaraderie of others. There's something special about moving together, sharing the same space, and laughing over the occasional wobble or misstep. These shared experiences create bonds that are hard to replicate in solitary workouts. Pickleball is the new craze for retirees because it keeps you active, social, and fun! This might be your game if you want low-impact and little running.

Consider arts and crafts workshops if fitness isn't your cup of tea. Picture yourself in a sunlit room surrounded by paints, brushes, and fellow creatives. Whether you are a novice or a seasoned artist, these workshops offer a space to explore your creativity while making new friends. You might find yourself deep in conversation about the best way to mix colors or the latest art exhibit in town. The beauty of these workshops is that they cater to all skill levels, so there's no pressure to produce a masterpiece—have fun and let your creativity flow.

Cooking classes and group dining experiences are other fantastic options, the aromas of fresh herbs and sizzling vegetables filling the air as you learn to prepare a new dish. These classes often culminate in a shared meal, where you eat and enjoy lively conversation. It's a wonderful way to try new cuisines, learn new techniques and recipes, and find friends who share your love of food. Plus, there's something incredibly satisfying about sitting down to a meal you've prepared with your own hands and sharing it with others. Check out **Tripadvisor.com** for a listing near you.

Many community programs are free or low-cost. Community centers often offer discounted rates for seniors, making it affordable to join multiple classes. Many courses are designed with seniors in mind, addressing accessibility. Look for classes with flexible schedules that fit your availability. Morning or afternoon sessions might be more convenient than evening classes.

Participating in group activities and classes offers many benefits. They provide structured social interaction, shared experiences, and learning and growing opportunities. You might also discover a new passion and make lifelong friends.

1.6 Finding Mentorship Opportunities

Mentorship opportunities can provide personal growth and help you feel connected. They are a fantastic way to stay engaged and make a difference. Sharing your professional or personal experiences with younger generations can be incredibly fulfilling. You can pass on your wisdom, guide others, and gain new perspectives. Being a mentor doesn't just benefit the mentee but enriches your life, too. It can help you build meaningful, long-term relationships and give you a sense of purpose.

Finding and joining these groups can be done by consulting healthcare providers or local hospitals. They often have information on various support groups and can point you in the right direction. Online directories and resources are also invaluable. Don't underestimate the power of church organizations, even if you aren't religious. They frequently host or know of groups you may be interested in.

As a mentor, you get to share your hard-earned knowledge and see someone grow because of your guidance. It's a deeply satisfying experience. You gain new perspectives and learn from the younger generation, which can be incredibly refreshing. So, take the plunge. Look into sharing your wisdom and see the immense value you offer. Contact healthcare providers, search online directories, and ask at community centers. You'll find that these connections provide emotional support and contribute to your personal growth. Check off the ones that interest you.

Bucket List Opportunities:

- Social Clubs or Organizations

- Hosting or Attending Local Gatherings

- Volunteer Opportunities

- Ways to Stay Connected

- Classes that Interest You

- Mentoring Opportunities

Chapter Two

Embracing Lifelong Learning

R emember when you tried to teach your grandkids how to use a rotary phone? The looks on their faces were priceless. Now, flip that scenario; what if you were learning something new and exciting, but instead of a rotary phone, it's an online course about something you've always been curious about? Welcome to the world of lifelong learning, where age is just a number and curiosity never gets old.

2.1 Enrolling in Online Courses

Online courses are full of knowledge and are right at your fingertips. You can sample a bit of everything, and the best part is you can do it all in your pajamas. The flexibility and convenience of online education are perfect for retirees. You can learn at your own pace, whether you want to breeze through a course in a week or take your sweet time over several months. There's no pressure—just learning. Whether you're interested in personal finance, health and wellness, or even creative writing, there's a course for you.

Finding the right online course can be as easy as pie. Websites like **Coursera**, **Udemy**, and **edX** offer an array of subjects. Coursera partners with universities worldwide to bring you top-notch courses you can audit for free or pay a small fee to earn a certificate. Udemy is like the Walmart of online classes—it's got everything from web development to yoga. Then, there's edX, which offers courses from institutions like Harvard and MIT for those who prefer something tailored for seniors, such as platforms like **GetSetUp**. They offer classes on technology, wellness, and even hobbies like photography. You can always learn a little about anything on YouTube, which is also an excellent resource for learning new skills. If you want to learn about a new hobby, there is likely a short video to get you started.

Many platforms offer step-by-step guides to help you navigate the sign-up process. If you get stuck, call their support hotline. Senior Planet, for example, has a free hotline to help you join classes and offers live help.

When it comes to choosing a course, the sky's the limit. Personal finance and investment courses can help you make informed decisions about your retirement funds. Health and wellness classes cover everything from nutrition to mental health, giving you the tools to live your best life. Creative writing and art appreciation courses can awaken your inner artist and provide a new outlet for self-expression. Online learning allows you to explore whatever piques your interest, from ancient history to modern technology.

So, what are you waiting for? Discover something new today! Whether you're mastering the stock market, improving your yoga poses, or writing the next great American novel, there's a course out there waiting for you.

2.2 Attending Local Workshops and Seminars

There's something extraordinary about the energy of a room full of people eager to learn. Local workshops and seminars offer a unique blend of hands-on learning and social interaction that online courses can't match. Picture yourself in a craft workshop, surrounded by others who share your passion for creating. You're not just learning a new skill; you're making friends, sharing laughs, and swapping a few stories. The immediate instructor feedback and the opportunity to ask questions on the spot can make a difference. Plus, the hands-on activities ensure you're not just sitting and listening—you're actively engaged, making the experience both educational and enjoyable.

The variety of topics available in local workshops and seminars is staggering. If you're crafty, you'll find plenty of DIY workshops that teach everything from pottery to quilting. These sessions are perfect for those who love working with their hands and creating something tangible. Health seminars and wellness retreats are also popular and incredibly beneficial. Many weekend seminars offer a chance to learn about nutrition, fitness, and mental well-being while meeting new people who share your commitment to a healthy lifestyle. Technology and social media classes are fantastic options. These workshops can help you get the most out of your smartphone, navigate social media, or even learn how to code.

Attending local workshops and seminars is a fantastic way to continue learning while enjoying the benefits of social interaction. These events offer a rich, engaging experience that enhances your life in countless ways. So, the next time you see a flyer for a local workshop or seminar, why not try it? You might find your new favorite hobby or meet a new best friend.

2.3 Book Clubs and Discussion Groups

Book clubs and discussion groups keep minds sharp while enjoying the company of others. They encourage regular reading habits, which can bring joy to our lives. There's something special about hearing diverse perspectives, which can open your eyes to new interpretations and ideas you might not have considered. These groups also help build community and belonging, making you feel connected and engaged.

Finding or starting a book club is easier than you think. Local libraries and bookstores are great starting points. They often host or can point you to existing book clubs that welcome new members. Online platforms like **Goodreads** also offer virtual book clubs, allowing you to join discussions from your home. Consider starting your own book club if you prefer a more personal touch. Hosting book club meetings at home can be as simple as inviting friends, setting a date, and choosing a book.

There are many formats for book clubs, ensuring something for everyone. Genre-specific clubs are famous and focus on particular types of books like mysteries, historical fiction, or nonfiction. If you have a favorite genre, joining one of these clubs can be a great way to dive deeper into the subjects you love. Themed clubs, on the other hand, might focus on broader themes such as travel, biographies, or classic literature, offering a mix of genres that revolve around a central topic. Online and in-person hybrid models provide the flexibility to take part in virtual and face-to-face discussions, catering to those with varying schedules or mobility concerns.

Incorporating book clubs and discussion groups into your routine can significantly enrich your retirement life. They provide intellectual stimulation, foster social connections, and offer a structured way to explore new ideas and perspectives. You'll find that these groups offer a fulfilling and engaging way to spend your time. Start by checking out your local library, browsing online platforms, or gathering a few friends to kick off your book club adventure. The stories and discussions await, ready to add a new chapter to your retirement.

2.4 Exploring Educational Travel Programs

Contemplate strolling through the ancient ruins of Pompeii with an expert historian narrating tales of the past or exploring the Serengeti's wildlife with a seasoned naturalist. Educational travel offers these enriching experiences and more, blending the joy of travel with the thrill of learning. It's not just about seeing fresh places; it's about delving into their histories, cultures, and natural wonders. Picture yourself on a guided tour, where each landmark holds a story, and every artifact reveals secrets of bygone eras. This kind of travel allows you to combine leisure with education, making your trip a journey of discovery and personal growth. Whether you're passionate about history, nature, or art, there's an educational travel program that caters to your interests.

Finding the right educational travel program is just a few clicks away, as is chatting with your local travel agent. Organizations like **Road Scholar** and **Smithsonian Journeys** are pioneers in this field, offering many learning adventures tailored for seniors. For instance, Road Scholar provides programs ranging from historical tours and archaeological digs to nature and wildlife expeditions. They even offer "Choose Your Pace" tours so you can match your physical comfort level. They have special trips where you can take your grandchildren; otherwise, they are adult trips. They have solo trips, including men only and women only. Road Scholar offers unique learning experiences led by experts, giving people exceptional opportunities to discover new things. These adventures unite people, encouraging conversation and building friendships while making learning a lifelong journey.

The variety of educational travel options is staggering, ensuring something for everyone. Historical tours often include visits to ancient ruins, medieval castles, and historic battlefields, with lectures and guided tours that bring these sites to life.

Archaeological digs offer a hands-on experience, allowing you to unearth artifacts and learn about excavation techniques. If you're a nature enthusiast, wildlife expeditions provide an up-close look at the world's most fascinating animals and ecosystems. For those passionate about art and architecture, tours of famous museums, cathedrals, and architectural marvels offer a feast for the eyes and the mind. Each option provides a unique way to learn while exploring the world.

With all travel, look for senior discounts, which many travel organizations offer. Booking trips during off-peak seasons can also save you a bundle. Here is some information you can research to get the best flight rates based on current insights from various trusted sources.

- **Google Flights** is praised for its price prediction, tracking features, and ease of use, making it one of the best flight search tools.

- **Kayak** is known for searching hundreds of websites and booking platforms for the best deals. It's good at finding flexible dates and multiple flight options.

- **Momondo** also offers real-time price comparisons and is a go-to for finding the cheapest fares.

- **Kiwi** is excellent for booking multi-leg trips and combining separate tickets for cheaper flights.

- **Expedia** is a sound choice for those seeking booking rewards, particularly for OneKey rewards members.

Booking directly with the airline often makes it easier to manage reservations and luggage. Many airlines offer a 24-hour cancellation window and a full refund.

Regarding flight pricing trends, many commonly suggest that airlines offer cheaper flights on Tuesdays, Wednesdays, and Saturdays and that they tend to be more expensive on Fridays and Sundays. Some studies support that booking around 28 to 44 days before departure is optimal, though the results can vary.

Many programs also offer accessible accommodations and activities. When selecting a trip, consider your physical comfort and choose one that matches your abilities. Travel anxiety is another common issue, especially if you're venturing into unfamiliar territory. Make a checklist of essentials, from medications to travel documents, and ensure you have everything you need well in advance. Consulting with your doctor before embarking on a trip can also provide peace of mind.

2.5 Learning a New Language

Picture yourself sitting in a quaint café in Paris, effortlessly ordering a croissant and coffee in flawless French. Or, perhaps you're at a bustling market in Mexico, haggling over the price of a beautiful handmade blanket in perfect Spanish. Learning a new language can open up a world of travel possibilities and keep your mind sharp and active. Learning new languages can improve memory and cognitive function. It's like a workout for your brain, keeping those neural pathways flexible and strong. Plus, it offers a fantastic way to connect with new cultures and communities, making your travel experiences more prosperous and immersive.

Apps like **Duolingo**, **Babbel**, and **Rosetta Stone** make language learning fun and interactive. Duolingo, for instance, turns learning into a game with levels to complete and rewards to earn. Babbel offers practical conversation skills that are perfect for those who want to start speaking immediately. Rosetta Stone uses immersive techniques, helping you think in the new language rather than translating in your head. If you prefer a more traditional approach, many community colleges and adult education centers offer language classes. These provide structured learning with the added benefit of face-to-face interaction. Language exchange groups are another fantastic resource. These groups pair you with native speakers who want to learn your language, offering a mutually beneficial arrangement. You teach them English; they teach you their language. It's a win-win!

Learning methods vary widely, ensuring there's something for every learning style. Audio courses and podcasts are great for auditory learners. You can listen while you're driving, cooking, or even gardening. They're a fantastic way to make the most of your time. Language immersion programs take things to the next level. Spending a few weeks in a country where your new language is spoken, attending classes, and practicing with locals can change your life. It's an intense but highly effective way to learn. Online tutor sessions offer personalized instruction. Websites like **Italki** connect you with tutors worldwide, allowing you to schedule lessons that fit your timetable. These sessions provide the one-on-one attention that can make a big difference in your progress.

Finding language partners for conversation practice can also help. Many language apps and websites offer forums or matchmaking services to connect learners. Practicing with a partner adds a social element, making learning more enjoyable. Language learning games and flashcards can also be incredibly effective. They make repetition fun and help reinforce vocabulary and grammar rules.

2.6 Pursuing Certifications and Diplomas

Formal education in retirement can provide a profound sense of achievement and open doors to new opportunities. It's not just about adding letters after your name; it's about gaining specialized knowledge and skills to make you more valuable in volunteer or part-time jobs. Perhaps you've always wanted to dive deep into nutrition and become a certified health coach, or maybe you've dreamt of mastering graphic design. Achieving these certifications fosters personal fulfillment, helps you set new goals, and keeps your mind engaged.

Finding and enrolling in certification programs is easier than ever. University extension programs and community colleges are excellent places to start. These institutions often offer a variety of courses aimed at retirees, with flexible schedules and a focus on practical skills. Online certification platforms such as Coursera and Udemy provide another avenue. They offer many professional courses you can take at your own pace. Industry-specific associations also provide certification programs tailored to particular fields. For example, if you're interested in project management, the **Project Management Institute** offers courses that can boost your credentials. These programs are accessible, providing step-by-step instructions on enrollment and course navigation.

Becoming a yoga instructor (check out **Yoga Alliance**) or nutrition coach can provide personal benefits and opportunities to help others lead healthier lives. If you're inclined toward the arts, certifications in creative fields like photography or graphic design can be immensely fulfilling. Being able to capture stunning images or create beautiful designs with professional-level skills could lead to a side hustle, besides an immense sense of accomplishment. For those interested in more technical fields, professional skills certifications in project management or IT can open doors to part-time consulting or volunteer positions requiring specific expertise.

Many programs offer flexible schedules, allowing you to balance learning with other activities. You might even find senior discounts through financial aid or scholarships. Ask about these options when considering a program. Taking a step-by-step approach can make even the most challenging courses manageable. Break down the coursework into smaller tasks. Support networks, whether study groups or online forums, can encourage and help you need to stay on track.

Pursuing certifications and diplomas in retirement is more than just an academic endeavor. It's a way to continue growing, set new goals, and find fulfillment. Whether diving into health and wellness, exploring creative fields, or enhancing other desired skills, there's a perfect program for you. So, go ahead—take that leap. You'll gain valuable knowledge and enrich your life in ways you never thought possible. Now, as we wrap up this chapter, let's get ready to explore the following exciting aspects of retirement: staying physically active and maintaining your wellness.

Bucket List Opportunities:

- Find an Interesting Online Course

- Attend Local Workshops

- Join a Book Club or Other Discussion Group

- Plan Your Next Trip

- Take a Class to Further Your Knowledge

Chapter Three

Physical Wellness and Exercise

Waking up each day with a sense of vitality, feeling refreshed and ready for whatever the day brings, isn't a utopian dream—it's entirely possible with a bit of dedication to physical wellness. If you groan whenever you have to bend down to pick something up, it is time to incorporate some gentle exercises into your routine.

3.1 Yoga and Stretching Routines

Yoga and stretching offer a bounty of benefits that go beyond physical health. They improve flexibility, reduce pain, and enhance mental clarity. These exercises make your joints feel looser, your muscles more relaxed, and your mind clearer.

For starters, they improve your range of motion and joint health. Think about how much easier it would be to reach that top shelf or bend down to tie your shoes. Gentle stretching can also reduce the risk of injury by keeping your muscles and joints limber. And let's not forget about stress relief. There's something incredibly soothing about yoga's slow, deliberate movements that help calm the mind and improve focus. Let's dive into some basic yoga poses you can do while seated. The Cat-Cow stretch is a fantastic way to start.

Sit with your back straight and feet flat on the floor. Place your hands on your knees. As you inhale, lift your chest and shoulders back, creating a gentle arch in your spine. As you exhale, round your back and bring your chin toward your chest. Repeat this a few times, synchronizing your breath with your movements.

Next, try the Forward Bend. If it works better for you, you can also do it seated. If you can't reach the ground, you can use a yoga block or keep your knees bent.

Sit or stand with your feet flat on the floor. Slowly bend forward from your hips, reaching your hands toward your feet. Hold for a few breaths, and then slowly come back up.

Finally, the Seated Twist is excellent for relieving tension in your back.

Sit with your feet flat on the floor and your back straight. You can place your right hand on the back of your chair and your left hand on your right knee or, as shown, hold your arms out to the side. As you inhale, lengthen your spine, then twist to the right as you exhale. Hold for a few breaths, then switch sides.

Stretching routines require consistency to see results. You don't need to spend hours each day, but incorporating short, daily practices can make a world of difference. Try to include these stretches in your morning or evening routine. Setting reminders to take stretch breaks throughout the day can also help. Whether you're watching TV or reading a book, take a few minutes to stretch your limbs and keep everything moving smoothly.

Here are some other stretches you can try.

Mobility issues or pain can make these exercises seem daunting, but there are ways to modify each pose to suit your abilities. For example, if you have trouble reaching your toes during the Seated Forward Bend, use a yoga strap or a towel to help. Loop it around your feet and hold the ends to assist your stretch. Using props like yoga straps or resistance bands can provide the extra support you need. Do your stretching with slow, gentle movements to avoid discomfort. The goal is to feel a gentle stretch, not pain.

3.2 Strength Training—The Panacea

There is ample evidence supporting the importance of strength training for older adults. Numerous research studies support the benefits of regular strength training. It can help maintain muscle mass and reduce the risk of chronic diseases such as heart disease, diabetes, and osteoporosis. Strength training has also been associated with a lower risk of mortality, as studies suggest that a few 30-minute sessions of strength training each week can reduce the risk of death from all causes, including cancer and cardiovascular disease, by 10–20%.

Strength training helps older adults maintain independence by enhancing mobility, preventing frailty, and improving overall quality of life. It also helps regulate blood sugar levels, supports a healthy body weight, and contributes to better mental health and cognitive function. Health professionals highly recommend seniors to incorporate strength training into their routine to improve longevity and preserve physical and mental health.

If you already have a regular workout routine, that is *good* for you; if not, there is no time like the present! Here's a basic full-body workout routine using dumbbells, with resistance band options for each exercise. Always start with a light warm-up (e.g., 5-10 minutes of walking or light stretching). If you are new to strength training, start with light weights and work up from there.

1. Dumbbell Squats

How to do it: Stand with feet shoulder-width apart, holding dumbbells at your sides. Bend your knees and hips to lower into a squat, keeping your chest up. Push through your heels to return to a standing position.

Resistance Band Option: Stand on the band, hold the handles at shoulder height, and perform the same squat movement.

Reps: 10-12
Sets: 2-3

2. Dumbbell Shoulder Press

How to do it: Sit or stand with a dumbbell in each hand, starting with them at shoulder height. Press the dumbbells overhead until your arms are fully extended. Lower them back to shoulder height.

Resistance Band Option: Stand on the band, hold the handles at shoulder height, and press upward.

Reps: 10-12
Sets: 2-3

3. Dumbbell Bent-over Row

How to do it: Stand with your feet hip-width apart, holding a dumbbell in each hand. Bend slightly at the hips, keeping your back flat. Pull the dumbbells toward your hips, squeezing your shoulder blades together.

Resistance Band Option: Stand on the band, hold the handles, bend slightly at the hips, and pull the band up toward your hips.

Reps: 10-12
Sets: 2-3

4. Dumbbell Chest Press

How to do it: Lie on a bench or the floor with a dumbbell in each hand and your elbows at 90 degrees. Press the dumbbells upward until your arms are straight, then lower them back down.

Resistance Band Option: Wrap the band around your back, hold the handles, and press forward as if performing a chest press.

Reps: 10-12
Sets: 2-3

5. Dumbbell Bicep Curls

How to do it: Stand with your feet shoulder-width apart, holding dumbbells at your sides. Curl the weights toward your shoulders, keeping your elbows close to your body. Lower the dumbbells back to your sides.

Resistance Band Option: Stand on the band, hold the handles, and curl them up as you would with dumbbells.

Reps: 10-12
Sets: 2-3

6. Dumbbell Tricep Kickbacks

How to do it: Hold a dumbbell in each hand, bend forward slightly, and keep your arms close to your sides. Extend your arms backward, squeezing your triceps, then return to the starting position.

Resistance Band Option: Stand on the band, hinge at the hips, and extend your arms backward, as with the dumbbell version.

Reps: 10-12
Sets: 2-3

7. Dumbbell Deadlifts

How to do it: Stand with feet shoulder-width apart, holding dumbbells in front of your thighs. Hinge at the hips, lowering the dumbbells to just below your knees, then return to standing by driving your hips forward.

Resistance Band Option: Stand on the band, hold the handles, and hinge at the hips as you pull up.

Reps: 10-12
Sets: 2-3

8. Planks (Core Stability)

How to do it: Lie face down on the floor, then lift your body onto your forearms and toes, keeping your body straight. Hold this position.

You don't need a resistance band for this exercise.

Hold: 20-30 seconds
Sets: 2-3

Cool Down:

Finish with 5-10 minutes of light stretching to cool down and improve flexibility.

3.3 Pickleball

If you remember your younger days on the tennis or racquetball court (or, like my husband, the volleyball court) and now the joints aren't cooperating, but you still enjoy these sports, then meet pickleball.

Benefits of Pickleball for Seniors

Pickleball offers seniors many physical and social benefits, making it an ideal choice for active aging. The game promotes cardiovascular health, improves balance and coordination, and strengthens muscles without the high impact of many other sports. Its pace is moderate, with a smaller court size and lighter equipment, reducing strain on joints and minimizing the risk of injury. Beyond physical health, pickleball is a social activity that allows seniors to connect with peers and engage in friendly competition, boosting mental well-being and preventing social isolation.

Basics of the Game

Players play pickleball on a badminton-sized court with a net that is slightly lower than a tennis net. It can be played singles or doubles, with players using paddles to hit a perforated plastic ball over the net. The game starts with an underhand serve, and the objective is to score points by landing the ball in the opposing team's court while preventing the ball from going out of bounds or hitting the net. Players typically play games to 11 points, although they must win by a two-point margin, and each team can only score points when serving. Pickleball combines tennis, badminton, and ping-pong elements, making it a straightforward game.

How to Find Games in Your Area

Thanks to growing popularity, finding pickleball games in your area is easier than ever. Many local parks, community centers, and recreation clubs now offer pickleball courts and open play times. You can check with your local **YMCA**, senior centers, or sports clubs to see if they host regular pickleball sessions. Online resources like Meetup.com, Facebook groups, and apps like **Pickleball Finder** can also help you connect with local players and discover nearby courts. The **USA Pickleball Association** provides a directory of places to play nationwide to help find courts and organized games wherever you are.

3.4 Swimming and Water Aerobics

Swimming and water aerobics offer a fantastic way to stay fit without stressing muscles and joints. The buoyancy of water reduces the impact on your body, making these exercises ideal for anyone dealing with arthritis or other joint issues. On top of that, water-based exercises enhance cardiovascular health, improving heart function and stamina. They also build muscle strength and endurance, so you can easily carry those groceries or lift your grandkids. Swimming can also reduce stress and improve mental focus.

First, if you don't have a pool at home, locate an aquatic center. Many community centers, YMCAs, and gyms have pools that offer lap-swimming times and water aerobics classes. Once you've found a place, familiarize yourself with basic swimming strokes. The freestyle stroke, or the front crawl, is excellent for beginners. It involves alternating arm movements and a flutter kick. The breaststroke, which is slower and more controlled, might be easier if you're just starting. Aim to swim for at least 20-30 minutes three times a week. This duration and frequency provide a good balance between getting a solid workout and allowing your body to recover.

Water aerobics classes are another excellent option, combining fitness with social interaction. These classes typically start with a warm-up, followed by exercises designed to elevate your heart rate and work various muscle groups. You might find yourself jogging in the water, doing leg lifts, or using water weights for resistance training. The beauty of these classes is that they cater to all fitness levels. The water's resistance makes each movement require effort, but the buoyancy helps you avoid the impact you'd experience on land. Plus, being in a group can be incredibly motivating. There's something about moving in sync with others that makes the time fly by and the workout feel less like a chore.

Use a flotation device, if needed, to boost your confidence. Noodles, kickboards, and flotation belts provide extra support and help you stay buoyant. If you're new to swimming, start with shallow water classes. These classes keep you in water that's usually waist to chest high, making it easier to find your footing and feel secure. Always consult your doctor before starting any new exercise routine, especially if you have health concerns. They can guide you on what activities are safe for you and any precautions you should take.

Water-based exercises offer excellent physical benefits and stress relief, perfect for maintaining your health and well-being. Plus, they provide an excellent opportunity to socialize and meet new people. So, whether you're swimming laps or joining a water aerobics class, take the plunge and enjoy the many benefits of water fitness.

3.4 Walking and Hiking Clubs

Walking and hiking are not just about putting one foot before the other—they are also about improving your health, lifting your spirits, and connecting with others. These activities are great for cardiovascular health, boosting heart function, and increasing stamina. Your heart will thank you for each step, and you'll feel more energetic throughout the day. Beyond the physical benefits, walking and hiking can work wonders for your mental health. Being outdoors, surrounded by nature, can significantly reduce stress and anxiety. Moving through a beautiful landscape can lift your mood and clear your mind. Plus, these activities offer ample opportunities for social interaction. Whether chatting with fellow hikers or joining a walking club, your connections can be incredibly enriching.

Community centers and libraries often have bulletin boards with information about walking groups. Once you find a group or start your own, creating a schedule and choosing routes is the next step. Aim to meet each week to stay consistent. When selecting routes, consider the group's fitness levels and preferences. Scenic urban walks through parks or botanical gardens are perfect for those who enjoy strolls. For a bit more challenge, beginner-friendly trails in local nature reserves offer a chance to explore while still being accessible. More adventurous, challenging hikes can provide a robust workout and stunning views.

Setting goals and milestones for the group can add an element of fun and achievement. Whether aiming to walk a certain number of miles each month or planning to tackle a specific trail, having goals keeps everyone motivated. You might even consider organizing themed walks, like a wildflower walk in the spring or a foliage walk in the fall. Themed walks add variety and give members something to look forward to. And let's not forget the social aspect. Post-walk coffee or lunch gatherings can be a delightful way to unwind and chat about the day's adventures.

Choose flat, well-maintained paths for easier access. Many parks and urban areas offer paved trails for those with mobility challenges. Invest in a good pair of walking shoes for comfort and stability. If needed, use walking aids like trekking poles for extra support. Safety should always be a priority. Stay hydrated by carrying a water bottle, and always bring a phone in emergencies. Letting someone know your walking plans is also a good idea, especially if planning a longer hike.

3.5 Tai Chi and Qi Gong

Tai Chi and Qi Gong are ancient practices that offer a gentle yet effective way to enhance balance, flexibility, and mental wellness. These exercises involve slow, flowing movements that help you find your center, both physically and mentally. People often describe Tai Chi as "meditation in motion" because it primarily improves balance and reduces the risk of falls. The deliberate movements help you become more aware of your body's position in space, enhancing your stability.

Beyond physical benefits, you'll find that these practices are fantastic for stress reduction. The rhythmic, mindful movements can lead to a state of mental clarity, melting away stress and leaving you feeling serene. And let's not forget about muscle strength and coordination. As you flow from one move to the next, you gently work your muscles, improving strength and flexibility.

Stand with your feet shoulder-width apart and your knees slightly bent. Imagine a string pulling you up from the top of your head, elongating your spine. Your shoulders should be relaxed, and your arms should hang naturally by your sides. Breathing is just as important. Inhale deeply through your nose, letting your abdomen expand, and exhale slowly through your mouth.

One beginner-friendly movement is the "Wave Hands Like Clouds". Start by shifting your weight to your right foot and lifting your left heel. Move your left hand across your body to the right while your right hand moves to the left as if gently pushing clouds. Shift your weight to your left foot and repeat the movement on the other side. This flowing motion looks beautiful and helps improve coordination and balance.

Qi Gong, closely related to Tai Chi, focuses more on cultivating energy—or "qi". One essential Qi Gong exercise for energy and relaxation is the "Standing Meditation". Stand with your feet shoulder-width apart and your knees slightly bent. Extend your arms in front of you as if you're hugging a large tree. Your fingers should be relaxed, and your palms facing each other. Close your eyes and focus on your breathing. Inhale deeply and feel the energy flowing into your body. Exhale slowly, releasing any tension. This exercise can be incredibly calming and rejuvenating, helping you connect with your inner self.

The benefits of Tai Chi and Qi Gong are best achieved with regular practice, but the rewards are worth the effort. Set aside a specific time each day to practice. Whether it's first thing in the morning to start your day with a sense of calm or in the evening to unwind, choose a time that fits your routine. Joining local classes or online sessions can provide additional guidance and motivation. Many community centers offer Tai Chi and Qi Gong classes specifically designed for seniors. Online platforms also provide many resources, from instructional videos to live virtual classes.

The good news is that these practices can be easily modified. If standing for long periods is challenging, you can alter many movements to be done while seated. Focus on slow, mindful movements that suit your abilities. Finding beginner-friendly classes or instructors who understand the needs of seniors can make a big difference. They can offer modifications and ensure that you're practicing safely. Start with slow, gentle movements to help avoid discomfort and ensure you get the most out of your practice without straining your body.

3.6 Home-based Fitness Programs

Do you want to roll out of bed, throw on some comfy clothes, and finish your workout without ever stepping outside? That's the beauty of home-based fitness routines. These programs offer unmatched flexibility and convenience. You don't need a gym membership, and there's no need to travel. You can exercise at your own pace and within your schedule. They are perfect for those days when leaving the house feels like a Herculean task. Plus, they're cost-effective. No expensive memberships or classes—just you, your living room, and maybe a few pieces of equipment. The barrier to entry is low, making it easier to stay committed.

Setting up a home fitness space doesn't require a lot of room or expensive gear. Start by choosing a dedicated space that's free from distractions. This could be a corner of your living room or even a spot in your bedroom. Make your workout area a little fitness sanctuary just for you. Next, consider some basic equipment. Resistance bands and light weights are versatile and don't take up much space. A yoga mat provides comfort and stability, while non-slip mats ensure safety during workouts. Even if you're working out at home, supportive shoes can help prevent injuries and make your workouts more comfortable.

An array of home-based fitness programs is available, catering to different tastes and fitness levels. Online video workouts are incredibly popular. Platforms like YouTube offer many free workout videos, from cardio to strength training to dance routines. Fitness apps like **Peloton** and **MyFit-nessPal** provide guided workouts and track your progress. Virtual fitness classes with live instructors add an interactive element, allowing you to join a real-time class from home. Printable workout routines and guides can be a great resource if you prefer a more structured approach. These will enable you to follow a set plan, making it easier to stay on track.

Continuous motivation can be achieved. Stay focused on your intentions. Start by setting realistic goals and tracking your progress. Whether aiming to complete a certain number of workouts each week or reaching a new personal best, having clear goals can keep you focused. Finding workout buddies or virtual fitness communities can also make a big difference. Sharing your progress and getting encouragement from others can be incredibly motivating. Scheduling regular workout times helps build a routine. Treat your workout time like an appointment you can't miss.

Home-based fitness programs provide a fantastic way to stay active without the hassle of leaving your house. They offer flexibility, convenience, and cost-effectiveness, making sticking to a fitness routine easier. By setting up a dedicated workout space, choosing the right equipment, and exploring the variety of programs available, you can create a fitness plan that works for you. And remember, staying motivated is all about setting goals, finding support, and building a routine. So, roll out that yoga mat, fire up a workout video, and enjoy the benefits of exercising in your home.

Bucket List Opportunities:

- Create a Fitness Goal

- Consider the Type of Exercise that Interests You

- Check Out Your Local Gym or YMCA

- Set Up a Home Gym

- Meet Up with a Friend to Walk

- Get Moving!

Chapter Four

Adventures and Local Outings

T ake a deep breath and feel the tension in your shoulders melt away. It sounds idyllic. Spending time in nature does wonders for your physical and mental well-being. Research shows that being outdoors can significantly reduce stress and anxiety. The natural surroundings act like a balm to your frazzled nerves, helping you feel more relaxed and at peace.

5.1 Exploring Nearby Parks and Nature Reserves

Want to stay fit and feel great? Try spending more time in nature. You will be surprised by the benefits. Activities like walking and hiking in parks and nature reserves provide excellent opportunities for physical exercise. They boost cardiovascular health, strengthen muscles, and improve flexibility. Plus, there's something incredibly refreshing about breathing in the clean air of a forest or meadow. It's like a mini vacation for your lungs.

Beyond the physical benefits, these natural spaces encourage mindfulness and relaxation. Walking through a park, listening to the rustle of leaves, and watching the play of light and shadow can be incredibly grounding. It's a perfect way to practice being present and appreciating the little things in life.

Finding local parks and nature reserves to explore is easier than ever. Start by using online maps and park directories. Websites like **AllTrails** and **Google Maps** can help you locate parks near you. These platforms often include user reviews and photos, giving you a sense of what to expect. Local tourist information centers are another great resource. They can provide maps, brochures, and insider tips on the best spots to visit. Ask friends for recommendations and check with local community groups. People you know often highly recommend the best places.

Once you've found a park or nature reserve to explore, you'll be amazed by the variety of activities you can do there. Bird watching and wildlife spotting are popular choices. If this is your jam, invest in a pair of binoculars and a guidebook of the various animals and plants to observe, and then see how many species you can identify. It's a peaceful, engaging activity that connects you with the natural world. Picnicking in scenic locations is another delightful option. Pack a lunch, find a shady spot under a tree, and enjoy being surrounded by nature.

Many parks also offer guided nature walks and educational programs. These can be a fantastic way to learn about the local flora and fauna. Knowledgeable guides lead these walks, providing fascinating insights into the ecosystem and its inhabitants. Choose parks with accessible trails and facilities. Many parks now offer paved paths and ramps, making it easier for everyone to enjoy the outdoors. You will want to make sure you bring all the supplies. Pack a water bottle to stay hydrated, a first-aid kit for minor scrapes and blisters, and a hat and sunscreen for sun protection. If crowds are a concern, consider visiting during off-peak times. Early mornings and weekdays are usually quieter, allowing you to enjoy the tranquility of nature without the hustle and bustle.

Nature Walk Checklist

- **Water Bottle:** Stay hydrated, especially on warm days.

- **First-aid Kit:** Be prepared for minor scrapes and blisters.

- **Binoculars:** Perfect for birdwatching and wildlife spotting.

- **Hat and Sunscreen:** Protect yourself from the sun's rays.

- **Comfortable Shoes:** Supportive footwear is a must for walking and hiking.

- **Map or Guidebook:** Know your route and points of interest.

- **Snacks:** Keep your energy up with light, portable snacks.

5.2 Visiting Local Museums and Historical Sites

Contemplate standing in front of a centuries-old painting, the colors still vibrant, each brushstroke telling a story of its own, or walking through a historical home, feeling the echoes of the past in every creaky floorboard and worn banister. Visiting local museums and historical sites offers a treasure trove of enriching and enjoyable experiences. These visits aren't just about looking at artifacts but diving into the rich tapestry of local history and heritage. You get to appreciate art and cultural artifacts up close, marveling at the creativity and craftsmanship that went into each piece. It's like a time machine for your mind, stimulating your intellectual curiosity and sparking conversations about life in different eras.

Your local tourism office's website will offer guides, often listing museums and historical sites worth visiting. These resources also provide details about current exhibits and special events. Many museums offer free admission days or discounts for seniors, so it's worth checking their websites or calling ahead to find out when you can visit without breaking the bank. Planning your visit around special exhibits or events can add extra excitement. For instance, a temporary exhibit featuring a famous artist or a reenactment of a historical event can make your visit even more memorable.

The variety of museums and historical sites available ensures something for everyone. Art museums and galleries are perfect for those who appreciate visual beauty and creativity. You can spend hours wandering through rooms filled with paintings, sculptures, and installations, each piece offering a new perspective. Historical homes and landmarks provide a glimpse into people's lives from different times.

Science and natural history museums are fantastic for those who love to learn about the world around them. From dinosaur fossils to interactive exhibits on space exploration, these museums make learning fun and engaging. Living history museums and reenactment sites take you back in time, with actors dressed in period costumes demonstrating what life was like in a particular era. These immersive experiences are educational and entertaining, making history come alive in a way that books and movies simply can't.

Many museums now offer ramps, elevators, and wheelchairs to ensure everyone can enjoy their exhibits. Taking advantage of free or reduced admission times can help if cost is a concern. If you prefer a quieter experience, consider visiting smaller, lesser-known sites. You may find new hidden gems without the crowds. Plus, the staff at smaller museums are usually more available to answer questions and provide personalized insights, making your visit even more enriching.

5.3 Day Trips and Scenic Drives

Day trips and scenic drives are the perfect way to explore new places and landscapes without the hassle of extensive planning or significant expense. These outings offer the freedom to go wherever the road takes you, whether a quaint little town, a stunning beach, or a winding mountain trail. The best part? You can take your time, stop wherever you want, and soak in the scenery. It's a leisurely way to spend a day snapping photos and creating memories without needing a plane ticket or hotel reservation. For those who love photography, these drives offer countless opportunities to capture the beauty of the world around you, from sunlit fields to charming roadside diners.

Check out websites like **Roadtrippers** or Google Maps, which can help you plan your journey, highlighting exciting stops. Packing essentials like snacks, water, and a first-aid kit is always good. You never know when hunger might strike or when a small blister might need attention. Be sure to check weather and road safety before you start. Nobody wants to be caught in a surprise storm or find out too late that a road is closed. Ensure your car is in good condition, with a full tank of gas and properly inflated tires. Preparation goes a long way toward ensuring a smooth and enjoyable trip.

The variety of destinations and routes available means there's something for everyone, no matter your interests. Coastal drives and beach visits are perfect for those who love the ocean. Picture feeling the sea breeze on your face and hearing the waves crash as you drive along a scenic coastal route. Mountain and countryside routes offer a different kind of beauty. Winding roads take you through lush forests and up to breathtaking viewpoints, where you can see for miles. Exploring nearby towns and villages can be just as rewarding. Each city has its unique charm and history, with local shops, cafes, and attractions to discover. Sometimes, you find the best experiences in the least expected places.

If you're interested in longer trips and scenic drives, these options are a fantastic way to spend your time:

Top 5 Scenic Drives in the U.S.

Pacific Coast Highway (California)

- Stretching along the rugged California coastline, this drive offers breathtaking views of the Pacific Ocean, cliffs, beaches, and charming coastal towns like Big Sur and Monterey.

- **Highlights**: Bixby Creek Bridge, Hearst Castle, and Santa Monica.

Blue Ridge Parkway (Virginia to North Carolina)

- Known as "America's Favorite Drive," this 469-mile route winds through the Appalachian Mountains. It offers stunning mountain views, especially in the fall when the foliage turns vibrant in the fall.

- **Highlights**: Great Smoky Mountains, Mount Mitchell, and various hiking trails.

Going-to-the-Sun Road (Montana)

- This 50-mile drive cuts through the heart of Glacier National Park, showcasing dramatic mountain landscapes, glaciers, and lakes. The winding road and sheer drop-offs make it thrilling for adventurers.

- **Highlights**: Logan Pass, St. Mary Lake, and Jackson Glacier.

Overseas Highway (Florida Keys)

- Stretching from Miami to Key West, this scenic drive crosses 42 bridges and 113 miles of islands. The turquoise waters of the Atlantic and the Gulf of Mexico provide panoramic views all the way.

- **Highlights**: Seven Mile Bridge, Bahia Honda State Park, and Key Largo.

Route 66 (Illinois to California)

- The historic "Mother Road" spans 2,400 miles across eight states, showcasing iconic Americana with roadside attractions, quirky diners, and vast stretches of the open road.

- **Highlights**: Cadillac Ranch, Wigwam Motel, and Santa Monica Pier.

Trains can also take you to exciting destinations, allowing you to relax and enjoy the ride. Check out these train trip options:

Top 5 Train Trips for Sightseeing in the U.S.

California Zephyr (Chicago to San Francisco)

- Known for some of the most scenic views in the U.S., this 2,438-mile journey travels through the Rocky Mountains, Sierra Nevada, and vast open plains.

- **Highlights**: Rocky Mountains, Colorado River, and Donner Pass.

Empire Builder (Chicago to Seattle/Portland)

- This Amtrak route takes you across the northern U.S., passing through the Great Plains, Glacier National Park, and the Cascade Mountains.

- **Highlights**: Glacier National Park, Mississippi River, and the Cascade Range.

Coast Starlight (Seattle to Los Angeles)

- Hugging the west coast for much of its route, this journey offers stunning ocean views, forests, and mountain vistas.

- **Highlights**: Puget Sound, Mount Shasta, and the Pacific Ocean coastline.

Grand Canyon Railway (Williams, Arizona to Grand Canyon)

- A short but iconic journey, this historic train takes passengers from Williams, AZ to the South Rim of the Grand Canyon.

- **Highlights**: Expansive desert views, the Kaibab National Forest, and the Grand Canyon itself.

Durango & Silverton Narrow Gauge Railroad (Colorado)

This historic steam train winds through the Colorado Rockies, offering breathtaking views of cliffs, forests, and mountain peaks.

Highlights: Animas River Gorge, San Juan Mountains, and historic mining towns.

These scenic drives and train trips offer a variety of breathtaking views, from coastal landscapes to towering mountains and iconic American landmarks.

5.4 Attending Community Events and Festivals

Do you love the thrill of a live concert, where the music vibrates through the air and everyone around you is dancing and singing along? Community events and festivals offer a treasure trove of social and cultural benefits. They're not just about entertainment; they're about connecting with others and immersing yourself in local traditions. Picture yourself enjoying live music, performances, and cultural displays, each one offering a unique window into the community's soul.

These events provide an excellent opportunity to meet new people and make lasting connections. Striking up a conversation with a fellow festival-goer is often as simple as commenting on the fantastic band playing or the delicious food you enjoy. Plus, you discover local traditions and customs you might not have known, enriching your understanding of the place you call home.

Finding and attending these events can be a breeze with a few practical steps. Start by checking local event calendars and community boards. Libraries, community centers, and grocery stores often have bulletin boards with flyers for upcoming events. Social media is another fantastic resource. Platforms like Facebook and Instagram teem with event announcements and pages dedicated to local happenings. Following these pages can keep you in the loop about everything from food festivals to charity runs. Don't hesitate to ask for recommendations from friends and neighbors. Word of mouth is often the best way to find the most enjoyable and lesser-known events.

The variety of events and festivals available ensures there's something for everyone. Food and drink festivals are a feast for the senses. They offer rows and rows of food stalls, each offering a culinary delight. You can sample exotic dishes, enjoy local favorites, and maybe even learn a new recipe. Music and arts festivals offer a different thrill. Whether swaying to a jazz band, admiring a street artist's work, or watching a theatre performance, these festivals provide a rich cultural experience. Seasonal and holiday events bring their charm. From summer fairs with games and rides to winter markets with handmade crafts and hot cocoa, these celebrations add a festive touch to any season.

If you are looking for a bigger festival opportunity, check out these:

Albuquerque International Balloon Fiesta (New Mexico)

When: Early October

Why visit: Watch hundreds of hot air balloons take flight at sunrise in one of the world's most photographed events. It's a peaceful, visually stunning experience perfect for retirees.

Highlights: Mass ascension of balloons, evening balloon glows, and cultural performances.

Mardi Gras (New Orleans, Louisiana)

When: February or early March (before Lent)

Why visit: Experience this famous celebration's vibrant parades, music, and food. For a more relaxed experience, retirees can enjoy daytime parades and less crowded areas of the city.

Highlights: Colorful parades, music, local food, and lively atmospheres.

Sedona International Film Festival (Arizona)

When: Late February to early March

Why visit: Film enthusiasts can enjoy a week of independent films and documentaries in Sedona's beautiful red rock setting—a perfect mix of arts and scenic beauty.

Highlights: Film screenings, workshops, and discussions with filmmakers.

National Cherry Blossom Festival (Washington, D.C.)

When: Late March to mid-April

Why visit: Celebrate the arrival of spring by viewing the stunning cherry blossoms that line the Tidal Basin. This peaceful, scenic event offers cultural activities.

Highlights: Cherry blossom viewing, parades, cultural performances, and picnics.

Newport Folk Festival (Newport, Rhode Island)

When: Late July

Why visit: This historic music festival offers a laid-back atmosphere and features performances by folk, Americana, and indie artists. It is perfect for retirees who enjoy live music in a relaxed setting.

Highlights: Outdoor music performances by well-known folk and indie artists.

ArtPrize (Grand Rapids, Michigan)

When: Late September to mid-October

Why visit: This unique art festival transforms the city into a massive gallery featuring installations, sculptures, and visual arts. It is great for retirees who love art and creativity.

Highlights: Public art exhibits, interactive displays, and artist meet-and-greets.

Epcot International Food & Wine Festival (Orlando, Florida)

When: September to mid-November

Why visit: Retirees who love culinary experiences can indulge in food and wine from around the world while enjoying "Disney's Epcot Park in a more relaxed setting.

Highlights: International food booths, wine tastings, cooking demonstrations, and live entertainment.

Bristol Rhythm & Roots Reunion (Bristol, Tennessee/Virginia)

When: Mid-September

Why visit: Celebrate the birthplace of country music with a festival dedicated to roots music genres. Retirees can enjoy live performances and explore the historic town of Bristol.

Highlights: Live music performances, cultural exhibits, and local food.

Charleston Wine + Food Festival (Charleston, South Carolina)

When: Early March

Why visit: This festival, set in the charming historic city of Charleston, is perfect for retirees who enjoy fine dining and Southern hospitality.

Highlights: Wine tastings, gourmet food from top chefs, and cooking workshops.

Holland Tulip Time Festival (Holland, Michigan)

When: Early May

Why visit: Modeled after the famous Dutch flower festivals, this celebration showcases millions of tulips in bloom and Dutch culture in a picturesque, small-town setting.

Highlights: Tulip gardens, parades, traditional Dutch dance performances, and cultural events.

Attending festivals can be an excellent way to enrich your social life and have fun doing so!

5.5 Gardening and Visiting Botanical Gardens

Gardening offers a unique blend of relaxation, exercise, and education. Tending to a garden provides a peaceful escape from the hustle and bustle of daily life. The repetitive actions of planting, weeding, and watering can be incredibly soothing—almost meditative. It's a fantastic way to reduce stress and find a sense of calm. But here's the twist: gardening is a sneaky workout. Lifting pots, digging holes, and pulling weeds all count as physical exercise, helping to keep you fit and active without ever setting foot in a gym. And let's not forget the educational aspect. Learning about different plant species, soil types, and horticultural techniques keeps your mind engaged and sharp.

Visiting a local nursery can provide invaluable advice on what will thrive in your garden. Next, gather some essential gardening tools and supplies. Suitable gloves, a trowel, a watering can, and some quality soil are your starting essentials. Once you're equipped, it's time to plant. Start with easy-to-grow plants like herbs, which can be incredibly satisfying as they're quick to grow and helpful in the kitchen. Watering is essential; most plants prefer deep, thorough watering to frequent, light sprinkles. Regularly check your plants for pests or diseases and address any issues promptly to keep your garden healthy.

Visiting botanical gardens can be just as rewarding as tending to your own. These gardens are living museums, offering a feast for the senses and the mind. Local botanical gardens and arboretums are beautiful places to explore. Each visit reveals something new: a rare bloom or a beautifully designed landscape. Like rose or Japanese gardens, themed gardens explore specific plant types and design philosophies.

Many botanical gardens offer guided tours and a wealth of educational programs. These are fantastic opportunities to learn more about horticulture from experts and gain tips and inspiration for your gardening projects. Botanical gardens serve as living classrooms where you can learn about different plant species, habitats, and unique characteristics.

While many places have beautiful local botanical gardens, here are some of the most impressive botanical gardens in the United States, known for their beauty, diversity, and dedication to plant conservation:

1. New York Botanical Garden (Bronx, New York)

Why it's impressive: Located in the Bronx, this 250-acre botanical garden is one of the largest and most diverse in the world. It features over one million living plants, 50 gardens, a Victorian-style conservatory, and a 50-acre old-growth forest.

Highlights: The Enid A. Haupt Conservatory, the Peggy Rockefeller Rose Garden, and the Native Plant Garden.

2. Chicago Botanic Garden (Glencoe, Illinois)

Why it's impressive: This 385-acre garden is spread over nine islands and boasts 27 display gardens and four natural habitats. It's renowned for its innovative design and diverse plant collections.

Highlights: Japanese Garden, English Walled Garden, and the Waterfall Garden.

3. Missouri Botanical Garden (St. Louis, Missouri)

Why it's impressive: Founded in 1859, this is one of the oldest botanical gardens in the U.S. and is a designated National Historic Landmark. Its 79 acres contain lush gardens and one of the largest rare and endangered plants collections.

Highlights: The Climatron (a geodesic dome conservatory), the Japanese Garden, and the Linnean House (the oldest continually operating greenhouse in the U.S.).

4. United States Botanic Garden (Washington, D.C.)

Why it's impressive: Located near the U.S. Capitol, this garden is one of the oldest botanic gardens in North America. The conservatory is home to a stunning array of exotic and native plants, making it a hub for education and conservation.

Highlights: The Jungle Room, the Desert Room, and the outdoor National Garden.

5. Desert Botanical Garden (Phoenix, Arizona)

Why it's impressive: This garden specializes in desert plants from around the world, notably those native to the Southwestern U.S. Its 140 acres feature more than 50,000 plants adapted to arid climates.

Highlights include the cactus and Succulent Galleries, the Desert Wildflower Loop Trail, and art installations like the Chihuly Glass sculptures.

6. Longwood Gardens (Kennett Square, Pennsylvania)

Why it's impressive: With over 1,077 acres, Longwood Gardens is famed for its intricate water features, grand conservatories, and dazzling horticultural displays. It hosts a wide array of seasonal events and light shows.

Highlights: The Italian Water Garden, the Flower Garden Walk, and the Indoor Conservatory.

7. Huntington Library, Art Museum, and Botanical Gardens (San Marino, California)

Why it's impressive: This 120-acre garden is known for its themed gardens, including Japanese, Chinese, and desert Gardens. It also features rare plant species, art collections, and a research library.

Highlights: The Desert Garden, the Japanese Garden, and the Rose Garden.

8. Atlanta Botanical Garden (Atlanta, Georgia)

Why it's impressive: Known for its innovative plant conservation efforts, this 30-acre garden also has a stunning orchid collection and one of the largest canopy walks in the country.

Highlights: The Canopy Walk, the Fuqua Orchid Center, and the Edible Garden.

9. Fairchild Tropical Botanic Garden (Coral Gables, Florida)

Why it's impressive: Specializing in tropical plants, this 83-acre garden is a paradise for lovers of exotic flora. Its collections focus on rare palms, cycads, and fruit trees.

Highlights: The Tropical Flower Garden, the Rainforest Garden, and the Butterfly Conservatory.

10. Dallas Arboretum and Botanical Garden (Dallas, Texas)

Why it's impressive: Spanning 66 acres, this garden is famous for its seasonal floral displays, expansive lawns, and themed gardens. It's a popular spot for educational programs and family-friendly events.

Highlights: The Rory Meyers Children's Adventure Garden, the Margaret Elisabeth Jonsson Color Garden, and the McCasland Sunken Garden.

These botanical gardens are among the most beautiful and ecologically diverse in the U.S., allowing visitors to explore stunning plant collections and meticulously designed landscapes.

Of course, only some have a sprawling backyard or the physical ability to manage a large garden. That's where container gardening and raised beds come in. These methods are perfect for small spaces and offer greater control over soil quality and plant placement. A collection of pots on a balcony or patio can create a beautiful garden. Choose low-maintenance plants like succulents or native perennials that require less water and care. With the right tools and techniques, even those with limited mobility can enjoy a sense of accomplishment from nurturing a garden. Tools with long handles reduce the need to bend and stretch, while raised beds bring the garden to you, minimizing strain on your back and knees.

Gardening and visiting botanical gardens offer a rich tapestry of benefits. They provide relaxation, physical exercise, and endless learning opportunities. Whether cultivating a garden at home or exploring the beauty of a botanical garden, these activities enrich your life in countless ways. So, grab your gloves, pick up a trowel, or plan a visit to a local garden. When you find one you particularly like, consider membership. This not only offers a built-in way to support many causes, like gardens, zoos, and museums, but also provides exclusive benefits and opportunities to get involved in the garden's activities.

5.6 National Parks

If you love nature, national parks should be on your bucket list, and if you want something that isn't overrun with crowds, look at this curated list of lesser-known—but still stunning—adventures. These are U.S. National Parks that are worth visiting, offering gorgeous landscapes and unique experiences:

Great Basin National Park (Nevada)

Highlights: Ancient Bristlecone pines, Lehman Caves, and some of the darkest night skies in the U.S. Perfect for stargazing.

Why visit: It's one of the least visited parks, offering solitude and a range of landscapes from desert valleys to glacier-carved peaks.

Annual visitors: ~130,000.

Best time to visit: Late spring to early fall (May to September). Summer offers pleasant temperatures in the 70s-80s°F at lower elevations, while higher elevations stay cooler. Winters can be harsh with snow.

North Cascades National Park (Washington)

Highlights: Rugged mountains, alpine lakes, and over 300 glaciers.

Why visit: Less crowded than other Pacific Northwest national parks, it's a paradise for hikers and adventurers.

Annual visitors: ~38,000

Best time to visit: Late June to early September. Summer is the ideal time for hiking, with wildflowers blooming and mild temperatures (highs in the

60s-70s°F).

Congaree National Park (South Carolina)

Highlights: Largest intact expanse of old-growth bottomland hardwood forest in the U.S.

Why visit: Offers a unique ecosystem with opportunities to canoe or kayak through flooded forests and explore diverse wildlife.

Annual visitors: ~160,000

Best time to visit: Fall (October to November) and spring (March to May). The weather is cooler and drier, with temperatures ranging from the 60s-70s°F. Summers are hot and humid, with mosquitoes being a significant issue.

Isle Royale National Park (Michigan)

Highlights: Remote island park in Lake Superior, known for its wolf and moose populations.

Why visit: Ideal for those seeking wilderness adventures. With backpacking, kayaking, and scuba diving options, it's one of the system's most isolated and tranquil parks.

Annual visitors: ~26,000

Best time to visit: Mid-June to September. The island is closed from November to April due to harsh winters. Summer brings mild temperatures (50s-70s°F), and fall offers cooler weather and beautiful autumn colors.

Capitol Reef National Park (Utah)

Highlights: Striking rock formations, fruit orchards, and historic sites.

Why visit: Far less crowded than Zion or Bryce Canyon, Capitol Reef offers amazing geology, scenic drives, and opportunities to pick fruit in historic orchards.

Annual visitors: ~1.2 million

Best time to visit: Spring (April to June) and fall (September to October). Temperatures are pleasant (60s-80s°F) and avoid the extreme heat of summer, which can reach over 100°F.

Black Canyon of the Gunnison National Park (Colorado)

Highlights: Sheer, steep canyon walls, and dramatic overlooks.

Why visit: The narrow, deep canyon offers stunning views and fewer crowds than the more famous Grand Canyon.

Annual visitors: ~310,000

Best time to visit: Late spring to early fall (May to September). Summers are warm (70s-80s°F) but not too hot, making hiking more comfortable. Winters are cold with snow, making some areas of the park difficult to access.

Lassen Volcanic National Park (California)

Highlights: Active geothermal areas, including bubbling mud pots, hot springs, volcanic peaks, and alpine lakes.

Why visit: It offers unique volcanic landscapes without the crowds of Yellowstone.

Annual visitors: ~500,000

Best time to visit: July to September. Snow can remain at high elevations well into June. Summer temperatures are mild (60s-70s°F), perfect for hiking. Winters are harsh, with heavy snowfall.

Guadalupe Mountains National Park (Texas)

Highlights: The highest peak in Texas, ancient marine fossils, and desert wilderness.

Why visit: It's a hidden gem in the Chihuahuan Desert, perfect for solitude and exploration with extensive hiking trails.

Annual visitors: ~200,000

Best time to visit: Fall (October to November) and spring (March to May). Summer temperatures can exceed 100°F, but in the fall and spring, temperatures are much more comfortable (50s-70s°F), and the fall foliage is beautiful.

Voyageurs National Park (Minnesota)

Highlights: Water-based park with interconnected lakes and boreal forests.

Why visit: Best explored by boat or canoe, offering secluded camping spots and peaceful water adventures.

Annual visitors: ~250,000

Best time to visit: Summer (June to August). Temperatures range from 60s-80s°F, ideal for water-based activities. Winters are frigid, with temperatures frequently dropping below freezing.

Pinnacles National Park (California)

Highlights: Talus caves, rock spires, and an endangered condor population.

Why visit: It's excellent for hiking and climbing, with unique rock formations and diverse wildlife, without the heavy crowds of other California parks.

Annual visitors: ~200,000

Best time to visit: Spring (March to May) and fall (September to November). Temperatures are moderate (60s-70s°F), and wildflowers bloom in spring. Summer can be extremely hot, with temperatures exceeding 90°F, while winters are cooler but mild.

These parks offer incredible natural beauty and unique experiences for those seeking to explore lesser-known gems of the National Park system. However, if you haven't seen the big parks and don't mind crowds or prefer to join an organized tour, check these out.

Yosemite National Park (California) ~3.7 million annual visitors

Highlights: Famous granite cliffs such as El Capitan and Half Dome; Stunning waterfalls, including Yosemite Falls and Bridalveil Fall; Giant sequoias in Mariposa Grove; Diverse ecosystems ranging from alpine meadows to deep valleys.

Why Visit: Yosemite offers breathtaking landscapes with towering cliffs and waterfalls. It's perfect for rock climbing, hiking, and photography. The park's accessibility and wide variety of outdoor activities make it a must-see for nature lovers. The spring and fall seasons are magnificent, with wildflowers and foliage adding to the charm.

Glacier National Park (Montana) ~3.0 million annual visitors

Highlights: Over 700 miles of hiking trails, including the famous Going-to-the-Sun Road; Alpine meadows, glacier-carved valleys, and over 130 named lakes; Wildlife sightings, including grizzly bears, mountain goats, and moose; Stunning glaciers and rugged mountain scenery.

Why Visit: Glacier is known as the "Crown of the Continent" for its majestic alpine scenery. The park's glaciers, wildlife, and remote wilderness make it an adventurer's paradise. It's perfect for hikers, backpackers, and anyone looking to experience pristine wilderness.

Zion National Park (Utah) ~4.7 million annual visitors

Highlights: Towering sandstone cliffs, particularly in Zion Canyon; Iconic hikes such as Angels Landing and The Narrows; Lush vegetation along the Virgin River, contrasting with the desert landscape; Slot canyons, waterfalls, and diverse wildlife.

Why Visit: Zion is one of the most dramatic and accessible national parks, offering jaw-dropping views from scenic roads and hiking trails. The challenging hikes, such as Angels Landing, attract thrill-seekers, while more accessible trails make it great for families and casual visitors. The contrast between green valleys and red cliffs creates a stunning visual experience.

Grand Canyon National Park (Arizona) ~4.7 million annual visitors

Highlights: The Grand Canyon itself—a 277-mile-long gorge carved by the Colorado River; Overlooks such as Mather Point on the South Rim and the remote North Rim; Opportunities to hike into the canyon via the Bright Angel Trail or South Kaibab Trail; Scenic helicopter or mule rides to view the canyon's immensity from different perspectives.

Why Visit: The Grand Canyon is one of the world's most iconic natural landmarks; its sheer size and geological history make it a wonder of the natural world. Whether standing at the rim or descending into the canyon, the views are spectacular and awe-inspiring. The Grand Canyon also offers unique ways to explore it, from rafting down the Colorado River to helicopter tours.

These parks offer diverse experiences, from towering rock formations and canyon hikes to glaciers and iconic viewpoints. Their unique natural features and accessible activities make them some of the most popular destinations for outdoor enthusiasts.

Bucket List Opportunities:

- Local Parks

- Museums

- Festivals

- Botanical Gardens

- National Parks

Chapter Five

Creative Hobbies and Artistic Pursuits

C reative hobbies, like painting and drawing, aren't just about making pretty pictures; they're about finding joy, feeling accomplishment, and reducing stress. These activities can turn an ordinary day into something extraordinary, providing a canvas for your art, mind, and soul.

4.1 Painting and Drawing

Even if your last encounter with paint was while finger-painting in kindergarten, you're in for a treat. Painting and drawing can be incredibly therapeutic. Envision the stress melting away as you focus on each brushstroke or pencil mark. This mindful practice can significantly reduce stress, helping you feel more relaxed and centered. As you immerse yourself in your artwork, you'll find that your focus and concentration improve. The world fades away, and all that matters is the canvas before you. Plus, there's immense personal satisfaction in seeing your creative vision come to life. Each piece you create reflects your inner world, a unique expression of your thoughts and feelings.

So, how do you get started? Let's begin with some basic sketching techniques. Grab a good-quality sketchbook and a set of pencils—nothing fancy, just the basics. Start with familiar shapes—sketch circles, squares, and triangles to get a feel for your pencil and paper. Don't worry about perfection; the goal is to get comfortable with the tools. Once you're warmed up, try a basic still life. Arrange a few objects on a table, like a mug, an apple, and a book. Sketch their outlines, focusing on how light and shadow fall on them. This exercise helps you see the world through an artist's eyes, focusing on shapes, lines, and shading.

Watercolor painting is a fantastic medium for beginners. It's forgiving, versatile, and oh-so-satisfying. Start with basic watercolors, a couple of brushes, and watercolor paper. Begin by experimenting with washes. Load your brush with water and some paint and sweep it across the paper. Notice how the color spreads and blends. Next, try an exercise like painting a gradient. Start with a darker shade at the top of the paper, and gradually add more water as you move down, creating a smooth transition from dark to light. Once you're comfortable, challenge yourself with a landscape. Paint a sky with a wash of blue, add some green for the ground, and maybe a few trees or mountains. Enjoy the process, and let your creativity flow.

A whole world of mediums and styles is waiting for you. Acrylic and oil painting offer different experiences and results. Acrylics dry quickly and are great for layering, while oils give you more time to blend and work on your piece. You can experiment with both to see which you prefer. Styles like abstract painting free you from the constraints of realism, allowing you to play with colors and forms.

Conversely, realism challenges you to capture the world as you see it, honing your observational skills. Mixed media projects are another exciting avenue. Combine collage, ink, and paint to create unique, textured pieces. The beauty of art is that there are no rules. You can mix and match techniques to create something truly your own.

Many art stores offer beginner kits with everything you need to start. Daily sketching practice can also boost your confidence. Set aside a few minutes each day to draw something—anything. Over time, you'll see improvement, and your confidence will grow. Joining local art classes or online tutorials can provide guidance and support. Art instructors can offer valuable tips and feedback, helping you refine your skills. Online platforms like YouTube or **Skillshare** have countless tutorials that cater to all skill levels.

Whether you are sketching basic shapes, experimenting with watercolors, or diving into mixed media, each journey is filled with discovery and joy. So, grab that sketchbook, dip that brush in paint, and let your inner artist shine.

4.2 Knitting, Crocheting, and Sewing

Let's delve into the world of textile crafts. Knitting, crocheting, and sewing are not just hobbies; they are gateways to relaxation that can create a profound sense of accomplishment. The rhythmic, repetitive motions involved in these crafts can be incredibly soothing. Each stitch you make helps to melt away stress, leaving you feeling calm and centered. Beyond the mental benefits, these activities also improve hand-eye coordination and dexterity. The satisfaction of completing a project—a warm scarf, a cozy blanket, or a perfectly sewn pillow—is a feeling of pride and fulfillment. I love creating practical, handmade items that my loved ones can use and cherish. My personal bucket list includes a complete handmade wardrobe.

You'll need some basic supplies for knitting: a pair of knitting needles and some yarn. Start with a stitch like the garter stitch, which involves knitting every row. This stitch is perfect for beginners because it's easy to learn, and you can use it to make various items, like scarves and dishcloths. To crochet, you'll need a crochet hook and some yarn. The basic technique involves looping the yarn around the hook and pulling it through loops to create stitches. Start with a single crochet stitch, which forms the foundation for many patterns. Sewing requires more equipment—a needle and thread, fabric, and perhaps a sewing machine if you're feeling adventurous. Begin with easy projects like sewing a pillowcase or a tote bag. These projects are straightforward and give you a sense of achievement without overwhelming you.

When ready, think beyond blankets and hats; you might even like leather crafts. Many people enjoy making belts and wallets. Check out www.buc kleguy.com/kits-patterns/, where you can find starter kits.

While these crafts are often considered "women's" domain, you might be interested to know that men like Tom Daley, the Olympic diver, have become ambassadors of knitting and crocheting, often sharing their creations on social media. He highlights how knitting has become a way for him to relax and be creative. Men like Kaffe Fassett and Adam Brooks are also well-known in the knitting world, with Adam sharing how knitting helped him cope with stress and improve focus (The Crafty Gentleman).

Other examples include online communities like *The Crochet Crowd*, created by Michael Sellick and Daniel Zondervan. These communities teach crochet to large groups and popularize it as a gender-inclusive hobby. These platforms warmly welcome everyone, regardless of gender, encouraging men to embrace the craft and showing that crocheting is for everyone (Hooked Goodies).

In the meantime, here's a guide to crocheting a potholder:

Materials Needed:

- Medium-weight cotton yarn (cotton is best for heat resistance)

- Crochet hook (size H-8 or 5mm is recommended)

- Scissors

- Yarn needle

Steps:

1. Start with a Slip Knot:

Make a slip knot on your hook to begin.

1. Chain 26:

Crochet a foundation chain of 26 stitches. This will determine the width of your potholder. You can adjust the number of chains depending on how large or small you want your potholder.

1. Single Crochet (SC) Across:

Starting in the second chain from the hook, a single crochet is used across each stitch. This means inserting the hook, yarn over, pull through the stitch, yarn over, and pull through both loops on your hook.

You should have 25 single crochet stitches by the end of the row.

1. Chain 1 and Turn:

At the end of the row, chain 1 and turn your work to begin the next row.

1. Continue Single Crocheting:

Single crochet in each stitch across, then chain 1 and turn.

Repeat this process, crocheting back and forth, until your potholder forms a square (approximately 25 rows).

1. **Finishing the Edge:**

Once your square is complete, you can add a border to give it a finished look. To do this, single crochet around the entire edge of the square. When you reach a corner, single crochet 3 times in the corner stitch to create a rounded corner.

Continue crocheting around all four sides of the square.

1. **Add a Hanging Loop (Optional):**

If you'd like a loop to hang the potholder when you reach one of the corners, chain 8 and slip the stitch back into the same corner stitch to create a loop.

1. **Tie off and Weave in Ends:**

Once you've crocheted around the entire edge and finished the loop (if added), cut the yarn, leaving a small tail. Pull the yarn through the loop on your hook to tie it off.

Use your yarn needle to weave in any loose ends.

Your potholder is now complete! It's ready to be used or given as a handmade gift.

There are plenty of resources to help you along the way. Online platforms like **Ravelry** and **Lion Brand Yarn** offer various free patterns and tutorials, making finding projects that suit your skill level and interests easy. YouTube channels like Sheep & Stitch and KnittingHelp.com provide excellent video tutorials that guide you through the basics and beyond. Joining local craft groups or online forums can also provide support and encouragement. You can find fellow crafters in these communities who are happy to share their knowledge and tips.

Finally, start with small projects to build your confidence. As you complete each project, you'll gain the skills and assurance needed to tackle more complex ones.

4.3 Photography and Videography Tips

Photography and videography are lovely ways to document life's precious moments while enhancing your creative skills. These hobbies allow you to preserve memories you will cherish for years. Whether it's a family reunion, a grandchild's first steps, or your travels to picturesque destinations, your camera becomes a time capsule. Beyond documenting events, photography and videography open up a world of artistic expression. You can explore different styles, experiment with lighting and composition, and even dabble in digital editing to bring your vision to life. Plus, learning the technical aspects of these crafts can be incredibly rewarding. From understanding camera settings to mastering video editing software, there's always something new to learn.

Understanding your camera settings is fundamental in starting your photography and videography journey. Most cameras, including smartphones, offer a variety of modes, such as portrait, landscape, and macro. Experimenting with these settings is a great way to understand how they can enhance your photos and videos.

Here's a basic tutorial on camera settings designed specifically for seniors who are learning photography and want to capture great photos with ease.

Understanding Camera Modes

Most cameras have several shooting modes. The easiest to start with is **Auto Mode**, where the camera automatically adjusts the settings. However, learning a few key settings can significantly improve your photos if you want to gain more creative control.

- **Auto Mode**: The camera picks everything for you—ideal for quick, no-fuss shooting.

- **Program Mode (P)**: Similar to Auto, but you have more control over settings like the flash and ISO (explained below).

- **Aperture Priority (A/Av)**: You control the aperture (the opening that lets light in), and the camera adjusts the rest.

- **Shutter Priority (S/Tv)**: You set the shutter speed, and the camera picks the aperture.

- **Manual Mode (M)**: You have complete control over the aperture and shutter speed. This is great for more advanced shooting.

Camera Settings

Aperture (f-stop): The aperture controls how much light enters the camera. A **low f-number** (e.g., f/2.8) allows more light and blurs the background, which is great for portraits. A **high f-number** (e.g., f/16) allows less light but keeps more of the image in focus, ideal for landscapes.

Shutter Speed: How long the camera's shutter stays open to let light in. A **fast shutter speed** (e.g., 1/1000s) freezes action, like a bird in flight. A **slow shutter speed** (e.g., 1/30s) allows more light and can create motion blur, such as when capturing moving water.

ISO: ISO controls how sensitive your camera is to light. A **low ISO** (e.g., 100) is ideal for bright conditions, while a **high ISO** (e.g., 1600) is better for low light, like indoor settings. However, a higher ISO can introduce grainy noise to your photos, so use it cautiously.

Focusing

Most modern cameras have an **auto-focus** feature, which makes focusing easy. Point the camera at your subject, half-press the shutter button to focus, and fully press to take the photo. If you're taking pictures of a moving subject, look for a **continuous focus** setting (AF-C) that adjusts the focus as the subject moves.

Using Flash

The camera might suggest using a flash in low light. For softer lighting, avoid direct flash and opt for natural light. Many cameras allow you to turn off the flash or use a mode that reduces harsh lighting.

Composition Tips

Finally, a well-composed shot can make a big difference. Follow the **Rule**

of Thirds, which involves mentally dividing the image into a 3x3 grid and placing your subject along one of the grid lines or intersections. This gives the photo more balance and makes it more visually attractive.

Basic recording and editing tips can make a big difference in videography. Start by holding your camera steady with a tripod or bracing it against a stable surface. Regarding editing, free software like iMovie or Windows Movie Maker offers user-friendly tools to cut, trim, and add effects to your videos. Projects like creating a photo diary or a short film about a recent trip can be a fun way to practice your skills.

There are several excellent resources where you can find training or videos on how to make and edit home videos, ranging from beginner to advanced levels:

YouTube

YouTube is one of the best free platforms for learning video creation and editing. Many creators post step-by-step tutorials for video editing software, including beginner-friendly guides. Check out channels like:

- **Filmora**: Great for beginners with easy-to-follow tutorials on video editing.

- **Peter McKinnon**: Offers tips on filming and editing with a creative focus.

- **Adobe Creative Cloud**: Provides in-depth tutorials on Adobe Premiere Pro, one of the leading video editing programs.

Udemy

Udemy offers various paid courses that teach video creation and editing. You can find courses tailored to editing software like iMovie, Filmora, Adobe Premiere, and Final Cut Pro. Courses often have lifetime access, allowing you to learn at your own pace.

Skillshare

Skillshare offers numerous video editing classes, including beginner-friendly ones that teach the basics of shooting and editing home videos. These courses feature popular video editing software like Adobe Premiere Pro, Final Cut Pro, and DaVinci Resolve.

iMovie Support (Apple)

Apple's website provides easy-to-follow instructions and tutorials on creating and editing home videos using their software for those using iMovie. The tutorials cover topics such as adding transitions, music, and titles.

Local Community Colleges and Senior Centers

Many community colleges and senior centers offer workshops or classes on video creation and editing. These can be great if you prefer hands-on learning in a classroom setting. Some libraries also host free workshops on basic video editing. By exploring these resources, you can learn to film and edit your home videos, creating memorable content for family, friends, and personal enjoyment.

The beauty of photography and videography lies in the variety of subjects and styles you can explore. If you're a nature enthusiast, capturing a flower's intricate details or the mountains' vastness can be incredibly fulfilling. Wildlife photography, though challenging, offers the thrill of waiting for the perfect shot of an animal in their natural habitat. Portrait and candid photography allow you to capture the essence of your subjects, whether it's a posed family portrait or a spontaneous moment at a party. Travel and documentary videography, on the other hand, provide a unique platform to tell stories. They allow you to showcase the culture, landscapes, and people you encounter on your journeys, and in doing so, they help you grow as a storyteller. Each style offers its own set of challenges and rewards, keeping your creative juices flowing.

Equipment costs can be a concern, but you don't need a high-end camera. Smartphone photography is a fantastic and accessible option. Modern smartphones have powerful cameras that can produce stunning images and videos. To enhance your photos, consider using free or affordable editing software. Apps like **Snapseed** and **VSCO** offer a range of editing tools to adjust brightness, contrast, and color. If you prefer working on a computer, programs like **GIMP** provide robust editing capabilities without the hefty price tag.

Online courses and local photography clubs can provide valuable guidance. These communities are filled with experienced photographers who are more than willing to share their knowledge and tips. Websites like **Senior Planet** from AARP even offer courses specifically designed for seniors, covering everything from essential camera functions to advanced editing techniques.

4.4 Writing and Self-publishing Your Memoir

Writing a memoir is more than just putting words on a page; it's a journey of personal reflection and growth. It's a chance to reflect on your life and capture the moments that made you who you are. Memoir writing records your experiences and wisdom that you can pass down to future generations. Sharing these stories with your family and friends offers a way to connect on a deeper level, giving them a glimpse into your world. This process can also be incredibly therapeutic, helping you make sense of your past and find meaning in your experiences.

Starting your memoir might seem daunting, but it becomes much more manageable with some organization. Begin by outlining important life events and themes you want to explore. Think about the pivotal moments that shaped your life—the highs, the lows, and everything in between. Creating a chronological outline helps to give your memoir structure. Jot down your earliest memories and work your way forward, noting significant milestones and turning points.

Once you have your outline, begin incorporating personal anecdotes and reflections. Doing so will add depth and personality to your memoir, making it more engaging for your readers. Don't worry about getting everything perfect on the first try. The important thing is to get your thoughts typed out. Then, there are many new tools for refining and checking your text. Look at **Grammarly.com** to see which sentences need grammatical work.

Now, let's talk about the process of self-publishing. Once your manuscript is complete, it's time to format and edit. Formatting ensures your text is consistent and easy to read. There are also many options for formatting your text to look professional. A Google search will lead you to resources. If you want to do it yourself, use a standard font like Times New Roman or Arial, with 12-point size and double spacing. Break your text into chapters and add headings to make navigation easier.

Here are three effective options for self-publishers to format their manuscripts:

Microsoft Word:

Why: It's one of the most widely-used word processors, and many print-on-demand platforms, like Amazon KDP, accept Word documents.

Key Features:

- Easy formatting tools for headings, margins, page breaks, and table of contents.

- Wide compatibility with different file types (like .docx and .pdf).

- Track changes function and comments for easy collaboration.

Best for: Authors who are familiar with Word and need a straightforward option.

Scrivener:

Why: This software is designed for authors and offers powerful organizational features.

Key Features:

- Compile your manuscript into formats (like .pdf, .epub, .mobi, and .docx).

- Offers tools for structuring long projects and managing research, notes, and revisions.

- Customizable export options for different publishing platforms.

Best for: Authors who prefer an all-in-one writing and formatting tool.

Vellum:

Why: Vellum is known for creating beautifully formatted books with little effort, especially for self-publishing on Amazon or other platforms.

Key Features:

- Drag-and-drop simplicity for creating professional print and eBook layouts.

- Easily converts to Kindle, Apple Books, and print-ready formats.

- Comes with customizable style templates.

Best for: Authors looking for high-quality, professional formatting for both eBook and print.

These options vary based on your familiarity with writing tools and the level of customization you need for your manuscript.

Editing is necessary, so having someone else read your manuscript to catch errors and provide feedback is a good idea. Once your manuscript is polished, choose a self-publishing platform. **Amazon Kindle Direct Publishing** and **IngramSpark** are popular options that offer step-by-step guides to help you through the process. These platforms allow you to publish eBooks and print-on-demand paperbacks, giving your readers options. Marketing and distributing your book are the final steps. Create an author profile on social media and share updates about your book. Consider offering a few free copies to friends and family in exchange for reviews. These reviews can boost your book's visibility and attract more readers.

Choose a time of day when you feel most creative, and commit to writing for a set period, even if it's just 15 minutes. Seeking feedback from writing groups or editors can provide valuable insights and motivate you. Joining a local writing group or an online community can offer support and encouragement. If technical issues with self-publishing platforms seem daunting, don't worry. Plenty of online resources and tutorials guide you through the process. Websites like **Reedsy** and the Kindle Direct Publishing help center offer comprehensive guides on self-publishing, covering everything from formatting to marketing.

4.5 Pottery and Ceramics Classes

Pottery and ceramics offer a tactile experience that's both relaxing and satisfying. The act of creating something with your hands can be incredibly therapeutic. The focus required to shape and mold clay helps relieve stress, leaving you calm and centered. You'll notice an improvement in your fine motor skills and hand strength as you work. Each piece you create, whether a simple bowl or an intricate vase, offers a sense of accomplishment. It's not just art; it's functional, too. You can use the items you make or give them as cherished gifts.

Start with basic pottery techniques. Hand-building is a great place to begin. This method involves shaping clay using just your hands and a few tools. One basic technique is coiling, where you roll out long, snake-like clay coils and stack them to form walls. Another technique is slab construction. Roll out a flat piece of clay and cut it into shapes, then combine them to create boxes or other forms. For those feeling a bit more adventurous, wheel-throwing offers a different experience. It involves using a pottery wheel to shape the clay as it spins. Start with a small amount of clay and practice centering it on the wheel. Once centered, use your hands to shape it into a form like a bowl or mug. These foundational skills open the door to a world of creative possibilities.

The variety of pottery and ceramics styles is vast, catering to different tastes and preferences. Other types of clay and glazes can produce a wide range of effects. Stoneware, porcelain, and earthenware each have unique properties and uses.

Experimenting with these different materials can be a lot of fun. You might prefer the smoothness of porcelain or the rustic feel of stoneware. Pieces like bowls, mugs, and plates are always popular projects because of their functionality. They're practical and make great gifts. If you're more inclined toward art, sculptural pieces offer a chance to explore your creativity. Try creating abstract forms or figurines. Surface decoration techniques like carving, stamping, and glazing add another layer of creativity. These techniques allow you to personalize your pieces, making each one unique.

Access to materials and kilns can sometimes be a barrier, but plenty of solutions exist. Many local pottery studios and community centers offer classes that include materials and kiln time in the fee. These classes provide a structured environment with the tools and equipment. If you prefer working at home, consider using air-dry or polymer clays. You can harden these clays without a kiln by letting them air dry or baking them in a home oven. They're perfect for smaller projects and experimenting with new techniques. Online ceramics communities and forums can provide support and inspiration. These platforms have experienced potters who are more than willing to share tips, answer questions, and offer encouragement.

4.6 DIY Craft Projects and Workshops

The joy of crafting comes from the personal satisfaction of creating handmade items. Each project is a chance to learn new skills and techniques, whether you're making a candle, a piece of jewelry, or a decorative wall hanging. DIY crafts also allow you to create personalized gifts and home decor. There's something gratifying about giving a friend a handmade gift or seeing a piece you made proudly displayed in your home. There's something incredibly satisfying about turning raw materials into something beautiful and functional. You get personal satisfaction from creating handmade items that reflect your unique style.

Getting started with DIY crafts is fun. Gather essential tools and materials. A good pair of scissors, a hot glue gun, and a selection of paints and brushes are great to have on hand. For materials, look no further than your own home. You can repurpose everyday items like jars, bottles, and old fabric into beautiful crafts. Begin with starter projects like candle making or soap making. These projects are straightforward and provide a great introduction to crafting.

For candle making, you'll need wax, wicks, and molds. Melt the wax, add your favorite scent, and pour it into the mold with the wick. Let it cool, and voila! You've made your candle. Soap-making follows a similar process. Melt a soap base, add colors and scents, and pour it into molds. These projects are not only fun but also practical. You can use the candles and soaps yourself or give them as gifts.

The variety of DIY craft projects is endless, ensuring there's something for everyone. Home decor items like wreaths and wall art allow you to personalize your living space. Your next project could be a beautiful wreath made from dried flowers or a colorful wall art created from repurposed materials. Personalized gifts like photo frames and jewelry add a special touch to any occasion. Seasonal crafts for holidays and special occasions are also a lot of fun. Create festive decorations for Christmas, Halloween, or any holiday you celebrate. These projects bring a touch of handmade charm to your celebrations.

Online resources like YouTube and **Pinterest** offer countless tutorials and ideas. These platforms are filled with step-by-step guides and inspiration for every craft imaginable. Joining local craft workshops or online classes can also provide guidance and support. These classes offer a structured environment to learn new skills and techniques. Don't be afraid to try new things and make mistakes. Each project is a learning experience, and the more you experiment, your skills will grow.

Bucket List Opportunities:

- Photography

- Painting

- Drawing

- Ceramics

- Sewing

- Crochet or Knitting

- Woodworking

- Writing

Chapter Six

Technology Tips

U nderstanding technology may not be a typical bucket list item, but depending on how savvy you are with technology, this may be a topic you want to explore. Technology is here to stay, and we should pay attention to it as we age. Staying connected in retirement is often reliant on current technology. If you are already a pro, skim or skip this chapter. You can take this little assessment quiz to help determine if your technology skills need sharpening.

Smartphones and Tablets

- Can you set up and customize your smartphone or tablet (e.g., change wallpaper, organize apps, adjust settings)?

- Are you comfortable downloading and installing apps from the App Store/Google Play Store?

- Can you manage notifications, Wi-Fi settings, and mobile data usage?

- Can you connect your device to Bluetooth accessories (e.g., headphones, speakers)?

- Are you familiar with security settings (e.g., enabling fingerprint/face recognition, two-factor authentication, or updating software)?

- Can you upload data (e.g., photos, contacts) to the cloud?

Social Media Platforms (Facebook, Instagram, Twitter, etc.)

- Can you create and manage a social media account (e.g., set up a profile or update settings)?

- Are you comfortable posting updates, photos, and videos to your social media feed?

- Can you adjust privacy settings to control who can see your content?

- Can you interact with others on social media (e.g., commenting, liking, or sharing posts)?

- Are you familiar with using hashtags, tagging people, and joining groups or communities?

- Can you manage multiple social media platforms (e.g., switching between accounts while posting to various platforms)?

Video Calling and Virtual Meetup Apps (Zoom, Skype, FaceTime, Google Meet)

- Can you schedule a video call on Zoom, FaceTime, or Skype?

- Are you comfortable joining virtual meetings using a link or meeting ID?

- Can you use essential functions like muting, turning off your video, or screen sharing during a video call?

- Are you familiar with using virtual backgrounds or changing your display name in video conferencing tools?

- Can you schedule or host a virtual meeting, including sending invites to others?

- Do you know how to troubleshoot common issues (e.g., poor video quality, audio not working)?

Health and Fitness Apps (MyFitnessPal, Fitbit, Apple Health, etc.)

- Can you download and set up a health or fitness app and enter personal health data (e.g., height, weight, goals)?

- Are you comfortable logging food intake or physical activities into a health or fitness app?

- Can you sync your fitness tracker (e.g., Fitbit, Apple Watch) with your smartphone or health app?

- Do you understand tracking and interpreting metrics like calories burned, steps taken, or heart rate?

- Can you use guided workouts or available health plans in the app?

- Can you set and track fitness or health goals (e.g., weight loss, step count)?

Streaming Services (Netflix, Hulu, Spotify, etc.)

- Can you set up an account and subscribe to a streaming service?

- Are you comfortable browsing and searching for movies, shows, or music in a streaming app?

- Can you create playlists (for music) or save shows/movies to a watchlist?

- Are you familiar with using parental controls and setting up multiple profiles within a streaming service?

- Can you download content for offline viewing or listening?

- Can you cast or mirror streaming content from your device to a TV or smart display?

Scoring Guidelines:

You're at a basic level if you checked 1-2 boxes for each category. You're at an intermediate level if you checked 3-4 boxes. You're at an advanced level if you checked five or more boxes.

Basic: You can perform some tasks but might need help with others. You know how to access the basic features but need to be more comfortable navigating advanced functions.

Intermediate: You are comfortable using most of the features of your devices and apps. You can troubleshoot fundamental problems and use a range of apps confidently.

Advanced: You are proficient and comfortable with your devices and apps. You can customize settings, troubleshoot issues independently, and explore new apps or features easily.

6.1 Mastering Your Smartphone and Tablet

Let's start with the basics. Smartphones and tablets are like Swiss army knives—they can do a little of everything. Making and receiving calls is their bread and butter. Remember the days of rotary phones? It's kind of like that but without the dialing wheel. Just tap on your contacts, choose who you want to talk to, and hit the call button. Sending and receiving text messages is just as straightforward. Think of it as writing a quick note and passing it to someone without the paper. Open the messaging app, select the contact, type your message, and press send. Voila! You're already a pro at this.

Now, let's talk about the camera. These devices come with cameras that can rival professional ones. Open the camera app, aim, and tap the shutter button. You've just snapped a photo! The photo gallery is where all your pictures live. Open it, and you can browse your memories, share them with friends, or set them as your wallpaper. It's like having a personal photo album in your pocket, ready to share your memories.

Another fantastic feature is setting up email and calendar notifications. These apps can act like personal assistants, reminding you about appointments and important emails. Set up your email account, and you'll receive notifications whenever you receive a new message. The calendar app can help you keep track of birthdays, doctor's appointments, and even your daily walks.

Customizing your device is like decorating your new home. Adjusting the screen brightness and text size can make everything easier to see. Find your settings app, look for the display options, and tweak them to your liking.

You must set up Wi-Fi and Bluetooth connections for optimal use. Wi-Fi connects you to the internet, while Bluetooth lets you pair your device with other gadgets like headphones or speakers. To connect to the internet, open the settings app, find the Wi-Fi option, select your network, and enter the password. For Bluetooth, turn it on, and it will automatically search for nearby devices. It's all about making your device work for you, not the other way around.

Installing and organizing apps is another step in making the device truly yours. Think of apps as tools in your toolbox. Go to the app store, download the ones needed, and arrange them on your home screen for easy access. Enabling voice assistants like Siri or Google Assistant is like having a virtual helper. Once activated, you can ask them to set reminders, send texts, or tell jokes. Just say, "Hey, Siri," or "OK, Google," followed by your command.

You'll find a world of apps that can enhance your everyday life. Communication apps like **WhatsApp** and **FaceTime** are perfect for staying in touch with loved ones. WhatsApp lets you send messages, make calls, and even have video chats—all in one app. FaceTime is fantastic for video calls, making it feel like your family is with you, even if they're miles away.

Health and fitness tracking apps can help you stay active and healthy. Apps like MyFitnessPal track your diet and exercise, while Fitbit syncs with your wearable device to monitor your steps and heart rate. News and weather apps inform you about what's happening worldwide and tell you whether you'll need an umbrella tomorrow. Apps like **The Weather Channel** and **BBC News** are reliable choices. Entertainment apps like **Spotify** and **Kindle** provide endless hours of enjoyment. Spotify lets you stream music, create playlists, and discover new artists. Kindle turns your tablet into a portable library, letting you read books on the go.

Basic troubleshooting for common issues can save you a lot of headaches. The first step to fix any glitch should always be rebooting—turning your machine, phone, or tablet off and back on. You will be amazed at how many hiccups this simple step fixes. If an app isn't working, check for updates in the app store. Sometimes, the latest version has the bug fixes you need. Attendance at local tech workshops or online tutorials can make a tremendous difference.

Online tutorials and webinars are also fantastic resources. Websites like YouTube have countless how-to videos that walk you through every step. Creating cheat sheets with step-by-step instructions can be incredibly helpful. Write the steps for everyday tasks, like making a call or sending a text, and keep them handy.

Mastering your smartphone or tablet is entirely possible with practice and patience. So, dive in and explore all the amazing things these devices can do. Before you know it, you'll show off your tech skills and impress your grandkids.

6.2 Using Social Media Platforms

Can you easily share a photo of your blooming garden with your family in seconds or catch up with an old friend from high school without leaving your living room? If not, read on. Social media has made staying connected more accessible than ever. Platforms like Facebook, Instagram, and **X (formerly Twitter)** offer a way to keep in touch with family and friends, share life updates, and even join special interest groups and communities. You can post photos of your latest knitting project or share a funny story from your day, keeping loved ones in the loop. These platforms are not just for the young; they're a powerful tool for staying informed and engaged.

Creating profiles on these platforms is your first step. Start with Facebook, the most popular platform among seniors. Go to Facebook's website, click "Sign Up," and fill in the required information like your name, email, and password. Once your profile is set up, take a moment to understand the privacy settings. These settings control who sees your posts, who can send you friend requests, and what personal information is visible. Adjust these settings to your comfort level. Instagram, owned by Facebook, follows a similar setup process. It's more focused on photos and short videos.

X is perfect for quick updates. Creating a profile is straightforward: Provide your name, email, and password. Remember to upload a profile picture; it makes your profile more personal and recognizable. For security, upload a photo that doesn't look straight at the camera (like a driver's license photo) but shows you doing something you love, like looking at your dog.

Posting updates, photos, and videos is where the fun begins. You can write a status update on Facebook, share a link, or upload photos and videos directly from your computer or smartphone. Instagram is all about the visuals. Snap a photo, add a filter, and write a caption before posting. X limits your characters, so your updates must be short and sweet. Engaging with content is also a big part of the social media experience. You can like posts, leave comments, and share content on all these platforms. It's a great way to interact with friends and make new friends.

The variety of content available on social media is staggering. Follow pages and groups related to your hobbies and interests. Love gardening? There are countless gardening groups where you can share tips and photos. Are you interested in history? Follow pages that post fascinating historical facts and articles. Educational content and tutorials are also plentiful. You can find video tutorials on cooking, crafting, and even using social media more effectively.

Social media is also useful for event planning and RSVPs. You can create an event on Facebook, invite your friends, and keep track of who's coming. This feature is especially useful for family gatherings and community events.

Privacy and misinformation are common concerns. Be aware so that you can recognize and avoid scams and fake news. If something seems too good to be true, it probably is. Don't click on any links or share personal information. Legitimate requests for information will be using secure messaging. Managing privacy settings is essential. Regularly review your settings to ensure you know who can see your posts and personal details. Using social media mindfully can help you avoid feeling overwhelmed or addicted. Set time limits for yourself and take breaks if you feel stressed.

Incorporating these practices into your social media routine can enhance your experience and keep you connected with the people and interests you care about. So, create your profiles, share your photos, and join those groups. You'll find that social media can be a fantastic tool for staying connected and engaged, all from the comfort of your home.

6.3 Staying Safe Online: Privacy and Security Tips

You've probably heard stories about people stealing their identities or falling for online scams. It's scary stuff, but there's no need to panic. You can confidently protect your personal information and surf the web with a few steps.

Identity theft is a big concern. Keep yourself safe from someone getting ahold of your social security number or bank details. They could open accounts in your name, rack up debt, and leave you to clean up the mess.

Online scams are another danger. They often come in emails or texts, tricking you into giving away personal information. Never respond to calls, emails, or texts with your personal information. Hang up if you get a call like that, and then call your bank or credit card company directly and ask them if they are looking for information. They are most likely not, and this is a scam. Many nefarious people and groups are out there, so don't allow yourself to fall victim. Furthermore, don't feel embarrassed. These scams look like authentic communications from your bank, so guard against them.

One of the best ways to protect yourself is using strong, unique passwords. Never use "password123" or your pet's name. It's easy to remember, sure, but also easy to guess. Always create complex passwords that include letters, numbers, and symbols. There are password manager tools you can find with a Google search and look for reviews and features, cost, and downsides that allow you to create one strong password; then, they make all your passwords and store them, so you don't have to remember them. They will fill in your login information for you. Also, as a rule of thumb, don't use the same password for multiple accounts. That way, if one gets hacked, the others remain safe.

A strong password should follow these parameters to ensure security and

91

protection against unauthorized access:

Length: At least 12 to 16 characters (the longer, the better).

Complexity:

- Include a mix of **uppercase letters** (A-Z) and **lowercase letters** (a-z).

- Include **numbers** (0-9).

- Include **special characters** (e.g., !, @, #, $, %, ^, &, *).

Avoid common phrases: Do not use dictionary words, personal information (like names, birthdates), or common phrases (like "password123").

Randomness: Use a combination of unrelated words or characters to create unpredictability.

Avoid repeating characters: Don't repeat the same characters or use patterns like "123456" or "aaaaaa."

Passphrases: Consider using a passphrase—several random words strung together—which can be easier to remember but still strong if long enough (e.g., "PurpleHorse!3Jumps").

Unique passwords: To limit the risk of a breach affecting multiple accounts, use a different password for each account or system.

Phishing emails often look like they're from legitimate companies but have subtle differences. They might ask you to verify your account or claim suspicious activity. Always double-check the sender's email address, and never click on links or download attachments from unknown senders.

Setting up two-factor authentication (2FA) adds more security to your accounts. It requires a password and a second form of identification, like a code sent to your phone. This makes it much harder for hackers to access your accounts.

Using a password manager can also be a lifesaver. These tools store all your passwords securely, so you only need to remember one master password. They can even generate strong passwords for you.

Another essential step is installing antivirus software and keeping it updated. This software protects your devices from malware and other threats. Regularly updating your device software and apps is essential; most apps will alert you that they need updating. Updates also often include security patches that fix vulnerabilities.

Online scams come in many forms, but knowing what to look for can save you a lot of trouble. Phishing emails and texts are standard. They might ask for personal information or direct you to a fake website. Always be cautious with unsolicited messages. Tech support scams are another trap. You might get a call or popup claiming your computer has a virus. The scammer will offer to fix it for a fee or ask for remote access to your computer. Legitimate companies don't operate this way, so hang up or ignore these messages. Fake online stores and fraudulent advertisements can also trick you into spending money on non-existent products. Stick to reputable websites and read reviews before making purchases.

Building confidence in online security practices takes time, but it's worth the effort. Regularly reviewing your account activity can help you spot suspicious behavior early. Look for unfamiliar transactions or changes to your account details. Attending online safety workshops or webinars can provide valuable knowledge and practical tips. Many community centers and libraries offer these resources. Creating a checklist of regular security practices can keep you on track. This includes updating passwords, enabling 2FA, and checking for software updates.

Online safety is all about being proactive and staying informed. With these tips, you can protect yourself and enjoy the benefits of the digital world with peace of mind. Whether shopping online, connecting with friends, or exploring new hobbies, staying safe online ensures your personal information remains secure.

6.4 Video Calling and Virtual Meetups

Wouldn't it be great to be face-to-face with your grandkids, who live a thousand miles away? Seeing their smiles and hearing their laughter is so joyful. Video calling has become a fantastic tool for connecting with distant family and friends. It's like having them right there with you, even if they're across the country or the globe.

Beyond family catch-ups, video calls allow you to participate in virtual events and classes, making it easy to continue learning and engaging with others. Hosting virtual gatherings and celebrations is another perk. Wouldn't it be amazing to celebrate a birthday or holiday with loved ones, no matter where they are? These virtual meetups can significantly reduce isolation and loneliness, especially if you cannot leave the house often.

Getting started with video calling platforms is easier than you think. Zoom is a popular option. To create an account on Zoom, visit their website, click "Sign Up", and enter your email. Follow the prompts to set up your profile. FaceTime is integrated into Apple devices, so if you have an iPhone or iPad, you need to open the app and sign in with your Apple ID. Scheduling and joining video calls is straightforward.

In Zoom, click "Schedule a Meeting," set the date and time, and send the invite link to participants. When it's time for the call, click the link to join. Adjusting audio and video settings ensures clear communication. Before the call, test your microphone and camera. Ensure that you have good lighting on your face and adjust the volume to hear and be heard clearly. A successful video call experience involves a few steps:

- Find a quiet spot.

- Use a stable internet connection.

- Have a backup plan in case of technical hiccups.

Virtual meetup options are plentiful and cater to a wide range of interests. Virtual book clubs and discussion groups offer a platform to share your thoughts on the latest read or dive into stimulating conversations. Online exercise classes and wellness sessions keep you active and healthy from the comfort of your home. Picture yourself joining a yoga class or a meditation session guided by an instructor over a video call. Also, virtual game nights and trivia contests add a fun and social dimension to your evenings. Whether it's playing a round of bingo or competing in a trivia challenge, these activities bring people together in a lively and engaging way.

If you're experiencing audio issues, check your device's volume settings and unmute your microphone. For video problems, ensure that your camera is connected correctly and not blocked. Practice makes perfect, so don't hesitate to have a few practice calls with friends or family to build your confidence. Exploring features like virtual backgrounds can add a fun element to your calls. Chatting with your friends while appearing on a tropical beach or in front of a famous landmark is fun. These backgrounds can also provide some privacy by hiding your surroundings.

6.5 Health and Fitness Apps

Health and fitness apps can act like a personal trainer or wellness coach right in your pocket. These apps help you track physical activity and set fitness goals to manage your health. Monitoring vital signs and health metrics, like heart rate and sleep patterns, provides valuable insights into your overall well-being. Guided workouts and exercise routines tailored to different fitness levels make exercising at home easy and enjoyable. Whether it's a yoga session, a strength-training workout, or a stretching routine, there's something for everyone. And let's not forget about meditation and mindfulness sessions that can help reduce stress and improve mental clarity.

Getting started with health and fitness apps is a breeze. Begin by installing popular apps like MyFitnessPal, Fitbit, and **Calm**. MyFitnessPal is excellent for tracking your diet and exercise. Download the app from your app store, create an account, and log your meals and workouts. Conversely, you can sync Fitbit with a wearable device to monitor your steps, heart rate, and sleep. Open the app, set up your profile, and pair it with your Fitbit device for comprehensive tracking. Calm is perfect for those looking to incorporate mindfulness into their daily routine. Download the app, set up your account, and explore features like guided meditations and sleep stories.

Setting up personal health profiles in these apps allows you to customize your experience. Enter your age, weight, height, and fitness goals for personalized recommendations. Most apps also offer options to sync with wearable devices, enhancing the accuracy of your health data. Explore app features like workout videos, health tips, and community forums to maximize your experience.

Nutrition and meal-planning apps like MyFitnessPal and **Yummly** can help you plan balanced meals and track calorie intake. These apps often come with extensive recipe databases and meal-planning tools, making healthy eating easier. Sleep tracking and improvement apps like **Sleep Cycle** monitor your sleep patterns and offer tips to improve sleep quality. They analyze your sleep data and provide insights into how to get a better night's rest. Mental health and stress management apps like **Headspace** and Calm offer guided meditations, breathing exercises, and mindfulness sessions. These tools can help reduce anxiety, improve focus, and promote overall mental well-being.

Many apps offer step-by-step instructions or video tutorials to help you get started. Setting reminders can help you stay on track with your fitness goals. Schedule daily reminders for workouts, meal tracking, or meditation sessions to build a consistent routine.

Participation in the "app" communities can provide support and motivation. Join forums or groups within the app where users share tips, success stories, and encouragement. Knowing that others are on the same journey can be incredibly motivating.

6.6 Streaming Services and Online Entertainment

The variety of content available on streaming services is truly staggering. For movie buffs, there's a treasure trove of films spanning every genre imaginable. Enjoy a classic romance one evening and a thrilling sci-fi adventure the next. TV shows offer endless entertainment, from gripping dramas to lighthearted comedies. Documentaries provide an excellent way to learn about new topics, with options ranging from nature and history to true crime and science.

If you're a music lover, services like Spotify (integrated into your streaming device) offer an endless playlist of songs and podcasts. Explore genres, create your playlists, or listen to curated ones based on your mood. Live events and performances are another fantastic feature. Watch concerts, theatre productions, and even sporting events live from the comfort of your home. Educational content is also abundant. Platforms like **CuriosityStream** specialize in documentaries and series that feed your curiosity. Whether you're interested in ancient civilizations, space exploration, or culinary arts, there's something for everyone.

The costs can add up if you subscribe to multiple services. Consider bundling subscriptions to save money. Some platforms offer bundled deals, like Disney+ with Hulu and ESPN+, at a discounted rate. Free trials are also a great way to test a service before committing. Remember to set a reminder to cancel if you decide it's not for you.

Streaming services have transformed how we entertain ourselves, offering a wide range of content that caters to every taste and interest. Whether binge-watching a new series, listening to a favorite podcast, or exploring an educational documentary, these platforms provide endless entertainment options. With a little practice and exploration, you'll soon have a personalized entertainment hub that brings joy and relaxation to your daily life.

Bucket List Opportunities:

- Take the Technology Assessment

- Work on the Areas that Interest You

Chapter Seven

Volunteering—A Deeper Dive

Volunteering and mentoring benefit the individuals receiving help and enhance the well-being and happiness of seniors, fostering a more profound sense of contribution and belonging in their golden years.

7.1 Mentoring and Tutoring Programs

Imagine the joy of guiding a high school student through the complexities of algebra and witnessing that moment when the light bulb finally goes off. It's a feeling of fulfillment that only comes from helping someone overcome a hurdle. You might also find joy in mentoring young professionals, offering career advice, and sharing tips you've picked up over the decades. The sense of commitment and belonging you've had in your golden years is profound when you share your expertise and life experiences in support of others. Your contribution is invaluable and deeply appreciated.

Mentoring can also involve sharing life advice, not just personal development tips. You've navigated life's ups and downs; your experiences can be valuable to a person just starting out. You could teach a young adult how to manage their finances effectively or offer time management strategies that have served you well. Mentoring individuals in specific fields or interests, such as arts, healthcare, or business, can also be profoundly impactful. Your specialized knowledge can guide someone on a path they're passionate about but unsure how to pursue.

Start by visiting local schools and universities. Many educational institutions have programs that pair students with mentors, and they're always looking for experienced individuals to provide support. Another great resource is online platforms like **Big Brothers Big Sisters,** which pairs mentors with young people in need of guidance. Community centers and after-school programs are also excellent places to offer your help. These centers often run tutoring programs for kids who need extra study help.

Various mentoring and tutoring roles are available, ensuring there is something to suit unique skills and interests. If you're passionate about academics, you might enjoy tutoring subjects like math, science, or reading. Helping a young student grasp complex concepts can be incredibly fulfilling. For those with a wealth of professional experience, career mentoring can be a fantastic way to give back. Business, healthcare, or arts guidance can help young professionals navigate their careers. Life skills mentoring is another valuable area. Teaching financial literacy, time management, or even cooking skills can provide young people with tools they'll use for the rest of their lives.

Find a program with a flexible schedule that fits your availability. You don't need to commit to a long-term mentorship; starting with short-term or one-time sessions can be just as impactful. You might wonder if you have anything valuable to offer, but remember: your life experience is a treasure trove of wisdom. Participating in training or orientation sessions can help build your confidence. Many organizations provide these sessions to prepare you for your role and ensure you feel comfortable and supported.

7.2 Volunteering at Local Shelters and Food Banks

Volunteering at local shelters and food banks is more than just a way to pass the time; it's a lifeline for vulnerable populations. Your companionship and support can make a world of difference. A conversation can lift spirits and provide much-needed emotional support. Assisting with administrative tasks and fundraising efforts ensures these organizations run smoothly and can continue to serve those in need. Your role in community outreach and awareness programs is vital. You help build a stronger, more supportive community by spreading the word and educating others. Your efforts are making a significant difference in the lives of others, and that's something to be proud of.

Contact local shelters and food banks; volunteer coordinators are often eager to match your skills and interests with their needs. Consider browsing volunteer matching websites like VolunteerMatch or Idealist, which allow you to search for opportunities based on location and interests. Participating in community drives and donation events is another fantastic way to start. These events often need extra hands for organizing, collecting donations, and distributing goods. They're a great way to meet like-minded individuals who share your desire to give back.

Various volunteer roles are available at local shelters and food banks, ensuring something for everyone, regardless of your interests or social abilities. Serving meals and organizing food pantry shelves are straightforward yet impactful tasks. Know that each meal you serve or box you pack is going to someone in need. Assisting with intake and case management tasks can be fulfilling as well. You'll be helping individuals navigate the often complex support systems available, providing a helping hand when they need it most. If you have a knack for event planning, helping with fundraising efforts can be a great fit.

Organizing charity events or managing donation campaigns can significantly boost an organization's ability to serve its community. Volunteering in challenging environments, such as local shelters and food banks, can be heartbreaking and gratifying.

Remember to take care of yourself and seek support when needed. Self-care practices, like taking breaks and talking about your feelings, can help manage stress and maintain your motivation. Many organizations offer volunteer training programs that prepare you for the emotional aspects of the job. These sessions can provide valuable tools and coping strategies, ensuring you're equipped to handle the challenges that may arise.

7.3 Participating in Environmental Conservation Efforts

Setting out to a local park to plant trees in the crisp morning air sounds like an exceptional way to start a day. The sun peeks through the branches as you and a group of volunteers dig into the soil, each tree representing a small (but significant) step toward a healthier planet. Environmental conservation is not just about saving the earth; it's about leaving a legacy for future generations. As retirees, you have a unique opportunity to contribute to preserving natural resources and ecosystems. The sense of accomplishment and pride in your contribution is empowering and impactful. You are not just planting trees but shaping a better future for generations to come.

Protecting wildlife and natural habitats ensures future generations can enjoy the same natural beauty you have. Reducing pollution and promoting sustainability helps create a cleaner, healthier environment. Educating the community about environmental issues can inspire others to take action and make a difference. Supporting clean energy and recycling initiatives can lead to significant, lasting changes in how we consume and dispose of resources.

Finding and joining conservation efforts is easy. Start by contacting local environmental organizations and parks. These groups often have ongoing projects and always need enthusiastic volunteers. Platforms like **Earthwatch** and **Volunteer.gov** are fantastic resources. Earthwatch offers opportunities to participate in scientific research and conservation projects around the globe, while Volunteer.gov connects you with local and national parks that need help. Community clean-up events and tree plantings are another great way to get involved. Volunteers usually organize these events well, and they're an excellent way to meet like-minded individuals.

There are a variety of conservation roles available, ensuring there's something to suit different interests and abilities. Monitoring natural spaces and habitat restoration are perfect for those who love nature and don't mind getting dirty. Spend a day or two a month monitoring bird populations or working to restore a wetland area—each task contributing to the health of the ecosystem. Organizing and leading workshops can be incredibly fulfilling if you prefer a more educational role. You can educate others about the importance of conservation, share tips on sustainable living, and inspire a new generation of environmental stewards.

Another impactful way to contribute is to assist with recycling and waste reduction programs. You might help organize recycling drives, educate the community about proper waste disposal, or work on projects to reduce single-use plastics. Supporting clean energy initiatives and advocacy can also make a significant difference. This might involve promoting the use of renewable energy sources, advocating for policy changes, or educating the public about the benefits of clean energy.

Many organizations offer training and orientation sessions to help you get started. These sessions provide the knowledge and skills you need to be effective in your role, boosting your confidence and ensuring you feel prepared. You can also find roles with flexible schedules and minimal physical strain. Many conservation projects need volunteers for short-term or one-off events, allowing you to contribute without a long-term commitment.

Each tree you plant, each piece of litter you pick up, and each person you educate contributes to a healthier planet. So, why not take that first step? Contact local environmental organizations, review Earthwatch and Volunteer.gov, or join a community clean-up. You'll find that the rewards of conservation work go far. You will leave a lasting legacy for future generations, knowing that you've played a part in preserving the beauty and health of our planet.

7.4 Assisting with Community Arts Programs

Community arts programs are the heartbeat of local culture and offer a fantastic opportunity for retirees to support and promote the arts. By encouraging creative expression and cultural appreciation, you help foster community and belonging. These programs often provide arts education and workshops, opening the door for people of all ages to explore their artistic side. Your involvement can make these opportunities accessible to everyone, from young kids discovering their talents to adults reconnecting with their creative passions. Supporting local artists and cultural events ensures the arts remain vibrant and integral to the community. Enhancing community spaces with public art projects, like murals or sculptures, transforms ordinary places into inspiring environments that uplift everyone who passes by.

Finding and joining arts volunteer opportunities is simpler than you think. Start by contacting local art centers, galleries, and theaters. These institutions often need volunteers to help with various tasks, from setting up exhibits to organizing events. Platforms like **Americans for the Arts** and **ArtsWave** are also excellent resources. They provide listings of volunteer opportunities in your area, making it easy to find a role that suits your interests. Participating in community arts festivals and events is another excellent way to get involved. These events often require a small army of volunteers to run smoothly, and your help can make a big difference.

A wide variety of roles are available in arts programs. If you have a knack for teaching, consider leading art classes and workshops. Sharing your knowledge and passion with others can be incredibly rewarding—guiding a group of eager participants through a painting session and watching their initial hesitations give way to creative confidence. Assisting with event planning and coordination is another valuable role. These events require meticulous organization, from art shows to theatre performances. Your help with logistics, scheduling, and coordination can ensure everything runs like clockwork.

Promoting events, managing social media, and contacting the community can significantly boost attendance and engagement. If you enjoy interacting with people, volunteering as a docent or tour guide can be a perfect fit. Leading tours and providing information about exhibits allows you to share your love for the arts with others.

Many organizations offer volunteer training sessions to prepare you for your role. These sessions can equip you with the knowledge and skills, boosting your confidence and ensuring you feel comfortable and capable. Time constraints may concern, but plenty of short-term or one-time volunteer opportunities are available. These allow you to contribute without a long-term commitment, making it easy to fit volunteering into your schedule. Choose activities that you're passionate about, and you'll find the experience far more enjoyable and fulfilling.

7.5 Nonprofit Boards and Committees

Joining a nonprofit board or committee isn't just about attending meetings; it's about using your experience to make a difference. As a retiree, you have a wealth of knowledge that can provide strategic direction and oversight to organizations. Your expertise can help guide mission-driven initiatives, ensuring they stay on track and effectively serve their communities.

One critical role you might take on is assisting with fundraising and resource development. Fundraising is the lifeblood of nonprofits, and your experience can be invaluable in creating successful campaigns. You might help develop strategies for donor outreach, organize fundraising events, or even leverage your network to bring in new supporters.

Enhancing organizational governance and policies is another critical area with a significant impact. Your insights can help refine policies that ensure the organization operates smoothly and ethically. Additionally, building networks and community partnerships can expand the nonprofit's reach and influence. Your connections and ability to foster new relationships can open doors to collaborations that benefit everyone involved.

Finding and joining nonprofit boards and committees is more straightforward than you might think. Start by contacting local nonprofits and community organizations. They often have information on board openings and the expertise they seek. Platforms like **BoardSource** or LinkedIn are also excellent resources. LinkedIn provides tools and guidance for prospective and current board members, while LinkedIn's Board Connect feature helps match professionals with nonprofit board opportunities. Networking with friends, colleagues, and community leaders can also yield opportunities. Sometimes, the best way to find a board position is through word of mouth. Don't hesitate to express interest and let your network know you seek board positions.

You might serve as a board member or advisor, helping guide the organization's overall strategy and decision-making. If you have a knack for event planning, joining a fundraising or event planning committee could be a perfect fit. These roles often involve organizing galas, charity runs, or other fundraising events. Participating in governance and policy development allows you to shape the ethical and operational framework of the organization. Supporting marketing and outreach efforts can also be incredibly impactful. Helping with an organization's campaigns, community events, or public relations can significantly boost the organization's visibility and engagement.

Of course, there are potential barriers to consider. Time commitment is a common concern, but many boards offer roles with flexible schedules and commitments. You can often choose how much time you can realistically contribute, ensuring it fits within your lifestyle. Lack of experience might make you hesitant, but many organizations offer board training and orientation programs. These programs prepare you for your role, providing the knowledge and confidence you need to be effective. Additionally, mentorship and support from experienced board members can be invaluable. They can guide you through the nuances of board service, making the experience more rewarding and less daunting.

Each decision you make, and strategy you develop contribute to the betterment of the community. So, why not take that first step? Contact local nonprofits, explore professional sites like BoardSource and LinkedIn, and tap into your network. The impact you can have as a board or committee member is profound for the organization and your sense of purpose and fulfillment.

7.6 Organizing and Leading Volunteer Groups

Have you always been the go-to person in your family for organizing holiday dinners, summer barbecues, and even the occasional family reunion? Now, you can use that knack for coordination for something that benefits the entire community. Organizing and leading volunteer groups is a fantastic way for retirees to take on leadership roles and inspire others. You can coordinate community service projects and events or build and manage volunteer teams. The work is about more than just getting things done; it's about mobilizing people and creating a ripple effect of positive change.

Organizing and leading volunteer groups begins with identifying community needs and project ideas. Look around your neighborhood and notice what could use a little TLC. Once you've pinpointed a need, it's time to recruit and motivate volunteers. Start by distributing flyers, sending emails, or posting on social media. Personal invitations can be effective; people are more likely to join if asked.

Your organizational skills shine in planning and coordinating volunteer activities. Create a timeline and assignments, and ensure everyone knows their role. Keep the lines of communication open, and remember to provide the tools and resources.

Evaluating and celebrating project successes is essential. After the event:

- Gather feedback.

- Assess what went well and what could be improved.

- Don't forget to celebrate your achievements.

Various leadership roles are available, ensuring something suits different skills and interests. Leading community clean-up efforts or beautification projects can be gratifying—like transforming a neglected park into a vibrant, welcoming space. Organizing fundraising events and charity drives is another impactful role. From bake sales to charity runs, these events can raise much-needed funds for important causes.

Coordinating educational and outreach programs allows you to share knowledge and inspire others. Whether it's a workshop on sustainable gardening or a seminar on financial literacy, these programs can have a lasting impact. Another exciting opportunity is managing volunteer efforts for local events and festivals. These events, from art fairs to music festivals, often rely heavily on volunteers. Your leadership can ensure everything runs smoothly, making the event enjoyable for everyone involved.

Building partnerships with local organizations and businesses can also be a game-changer. They can provide resources, funding, and additional volunteers. This project takes a team-oriented approach, where everyone feels valued and responsible for the project's success. This lightens the load and fosters a sense of ownership and commitment among the volunteers.

Each event you organize, team you build, and volunteer you support contributes to a stronger, more connected community. So, why not take that first step? Identify a community need, gather a group of enthusiastic volunteers, and lead them to success. The impact you make will be profound, both for the community and for your sense of purpose and fulfillment.

Bucket List Opportunities:

- Find a Way to Use Your Gifts

- Food Banks

- Mentoring

- Board Participation

- Community Arts

Chapter Eight

Wellness

V isualize this: You're sitting on your porch, sipping a cup of tea, and feeling calm. The day's worries fade, leaving you with a sense of peace you haven't felt in years. That, my friend, is the magic of meditation and mindfulness. They aren't just for monks in the mountains or yogis on Instagram. They're for anyone seeking a bit of tranquility in their lives.

8.1 Meditation and Mindfulness Practices

Meditation and mindfulness aren't just buzzwords. They're powerful tools for reducing stress, improving focus, and enhancing overall well-being. Being able to calm your mind at will allows you to lower anxiety and depression with a few deep breaths. It's no secret that meditation can significantly improve emotional regulation, helping you respond gracefully to life's ups and downs. Meditation improves concentration and mental clarity, making those "senior moments" less frequent. And let's not forget better sleep quality. A few minutes of mindfulness before bed can work wonders for your rest.

Starting a meditation practice doesn't require a trip to a monastery. You can begin right in your living room. Choose a quiet, comfortable space without being disturbed, such as a cozy corner with a comfy chair or a sunny spot by the window. Set a regular meditation schedule. Think of it as an appointment with yourself that you can't miss. Start with short sessions, maybe just five minutes, and gradually increase the duration as you become more comfortable. Guided meditation apps like Headspace or Calm are excellent resources. They offer sessions tailored to beginners, guiding you through the process with soothing voices and gentle instructions.

There are several mindfulness practices, so you're bound to find one that suits you. Start with mindful breathing exercises. Focusing on your breath, inhaling in and out slowly, will bring your attention back whenever your mind wanders. Body scan meditation is another excellent practice. Lie comfortably and mentally scan your body from head to toe, noticing tension and consciously relaxing each part. Loving-kindness meditation, or Metta, involves sending kindness and well-wishes to yourself and others. It's a beautiful way to cultivate compassion. For those who like to stay active, mindful walking or movement can be incredibly grounding. Each step becomes a meditation, bringing awareness to the sensation of your feet touching the ground and the rhythm of your breath.

Restlessness is common, especially in the beginning. It's normal for your mind to wander, but gently bring it back without judgment. Patience and consistency are your best friends here. Use mindfulness techniques throughout your day. When you start feeling stressed, pause and take a few deep breaths. Join local meditation groups or online communities for support and encouragement. Sharing your experiences with others can make the journey more enjoyable and less solitary.

So, if you're ready to find that inner peace, start with a few minutes each day. Choose a quiet spot, set a regular time, and explore different mindfulness practices until you find one that resonates with you. Remember, it's not about achieving perfection but finding a bit of calm in the chaos. Happy meditating!

8.2 Engaging in Brain Games and Puzzles

Imagine sitting at your kitchen table with a cup of coffee and a crossword puzzle before you. Each clue you solve gives you a little jolt of satisfaction. Brain games and puzzles are more than just fun; they keep your mind sharp and improve cognitive function. Engaging in these activities can enhance your memory and recall, making it easier to remember where you left your keys or the actor's name in your favorite film. They also improve problem-solving skills. You'll find yourself thinking more clearly and tackling challenges with greater ease. Increased mental agility is another perk, helping you stay quick-witted and on your toes. And the best part? These activities can delay cognitive decline, keeping your brain healthy as you age.

Incorporating brain games and puzzles into your daily routine is easier than you think. Start with the classics like crossword puzzles and Sudoku. These are great for honing your vocabulary and numerical skills. You can find them in newspapers, books, or online. Jigsaw puzzles and brain teasers are another excellent option. They require strategy and patience, making them a good way to spend a quiet afternoon.

For a more interactive experience, consider online brain training apps like **Lumosity** and Peak. These apps offer a variety of games designed to challenge different aspects of your cognitive function. Strategy games like chess and bridge are also helpful. They improve your strategic thinking and offer social interaction if you play with friends or join a club.

The variety of brain games and puzzles available is astounding, so there's something for everyone. Word games and trivia quizzes are perfect if you love language and facts. They challenge your memory and broaden your knowledge. Logic puzzles and riddles are great for those who enjoy a good mental workout. They require you to think outside the box and develop creative solutions. Memory games and matching exercises can be particularly beneficial. They help improve your recall and keep your mind agile. For something a bit more adventurous, try creative puzzles like escape rooms or mystery challenges. These can be done in person or online and offer a thrilling way to test your problem-solving skills.

Puzzle books and online resources offer endless options, so you'll always have new challenges. Websites like **Puzzle Baron** and **JigZone** provide various puzzles for all skill levels. Joining puzzle clubs or online forums can also be incredibly helpful. These communities offer support, recommendations, and a chance to share your achievements with others who appreciate the thrill of a good puzzle.

So, grab that crossword puzzle, download a brain training app, or set up a chessboard. These activities are not just a way to pass the time; they're a powerful tool for keeping your mind sharp and engaged.

8.3 Nutrition and Healthy Eating

Picture yourself sitting down to a meal that's delicious *and* nourishing. Balanced nutrition is a game-changer, especially as we age. Proper nutrition supports immune function. Maintaining a healthy weight and muscle mass becomes more critical as our metabolism slows. And let's not forget the big hitters—reducing the risk of heart disease and diabetes. A balanced diet can help you keep these chronic diseases at bay. Plus, good nutrition can enhance mental clarity and mood.

Creating a healthy eating plan doesn't have to be complicated—incorporate a variety of fruits and vegetables into your meals. Think of your plate as a canvas: the better the colors. First, choose complex carbohydrates such as brown rice, quinoa, and whole-wheat bread over refined grains like white bread, rice, etc. These options provide more prolonged satiety and are rich in nutrients. Then, add a portion (the size of a deck of cards) of lean protein such as chicken, turkey, beans, or tofu. There isn't a diet or meal plan that won't tell you to limit processed foods (think potato chips) and added sugars (cookies, cake, etc.). Do your best to stay clear of pre-packaged snacks and sugary drinks. Staying hydrated is necessary. Your go-to beverage should be water—try it with a squeeze of lemon. Herbal teas can add variety.

Seniors have specific dietary needs that require attention. Managing portion sizes and calorie intake is vital. Eating more than you need is easy, especially when portion sizes have grown. Check with your doctor to ensure you get enough calcium and vitamin D for bone health. Adapting meals for dietary restrictions (like low-sodium or gluten-free) doesn't mean sacrificing flavor. Use herbs, salsas, and spices to jazz up a meal. Senior-specific nutrition programs and resources, like the ones offered by community centers and organizations like **Meals on Wheels**, provide tailored advice and meal options.

If the grocery store is something you want to take off your to-do list, try meal delivery services and grocery delivery apps that can bring everything you need right to your doorstep. You'll learn new recipes and techniques while socializing with others looking to improve their diet.

Balanced nutrition is the foundation for good health and well-being. So, whether you're whipping up a colorful salad, trying out a new whole grain, or exploring various nutrition programs, you're making a choice that benefits your body and mind.

8.4 Sleep Hygiene and Relaxation Techniques

Do you dream about drifting off to sleep as soon as your head hits the pillow, waking up refreshed and ready to tackle the day? Good sleep hygiene can make this dream a reality. Proper sleep is essential for good physical health, cognitive function, emotional regulation, and the body's ability to repair and restore itself. Adequate sleep supports immune function, metabolism, memory, and mental health. Chronic sleep deprivation is a big deal because it can lead to several health issues, including heart disease, obesity, diabetes, and depression.

Healthcare experts emphasize that quality sleep is as essential as proper nutrition and regular exercise for maintaining good health. It improves mood and emotional regulation, helping you easily handle stress and anxiety. Enhanced cognitive function and memory are benefits, making recalling names, dates, and where you left your keys easier. Better physical health and immune function mean fewer colds and quicker recovery times. Plus, a good night's sleep increases energy and productivity so that you can fully enjoy your retirement.

Establishing good sleep habits starts with scheduling and waking times and making them consistent daily. Create a relaxing bedtime routine. This could include brushing your teeth daily, reading a little before bed, or taking a nightly shower. Ensure your sleep environment is comfortable. Your bedroom should be dark, quiet, and cool. Some people like to use blackout curtains to make the room dark and earplugs and white noise machines to cancel out sounds.

If you're having trouble winding down, various relaxation techniques can help. Progressive muscle relaxation involves tensing and slowly relaxing each muscle group. Gently tense each muscle group from head to toe. This technique can help release physical tension and promote relaxation, creating relief. Deep breathing exercises are another great option. Guided imagery and visualization can transport you to a peaceful place, like a serene beach or a quiet forest. You can also try a few drops of essential oils on your temples or in a diffuser to create a calming atmosphere.

If sleep problems persist, try keeping a log of your sleep patterns. Jot down when you go to bed, when you wake up, and how many times you wake up at night. Also, record what you eat and drink, your activities, and your stress levels to see if you notice any correlations. If insomnia or restless sleep persists, consult healthcare providers. Sleep apps and trackers can also be helpful, as they monitor your sleep patterns and offer insights and tips for improvement.

8.5 Finding Balance: Relaxation vs. Staying Productive

Balancing relaxation with productivity enhances overall well-being and satisfaction. It prevents burnout and stress by ensuring you're not constantly on the go. Time to relax can improve mental and physical health, making you feel more vibrant and energetic. This balance promotes a sense of accomplishment and fulfillment as you achieve your goals without sacrificing your peace of mind. Encouraging a well-rounded lifestyle helps you enjoy the best of both worlds—being productive while also taking time to unwind.

Creating a balanced daily routine involves setting realistic goals and priorities. Start by listing your daily goals, but don't overload your schedule. It's important to be kind to yourself and recognize that it's okay if not everything gets done. Schedule both regular breaks and leisure time for your best life. Think of these breaks as mini vacations for your mind and body.

Incorporate physical, mental, and social activities to keep things interesting. For example, you could start the day with a gentle walk, read a good book, and catch up with a friend in the evening. Practicing self-care and mindfulness can also help you stay grounded. Whether it's a warm bath, a hobby you enjoy, or simply sitting quietly with your thoughts, these moments of self-care are vital.

Feeling overwhelmed and lacking motivation can be significant barriers to finding balance. Using planners or apps to organize tasks and activities can help. There's something satisfying about checking things off a list. Seeking support from friends, family, or support groups can also provide encouragement and advice. Sometimes, just talking things through with someone can help. Practicing self-compassion and adjusting expectations is paramount to good health. Be gentle with yourself and recognize that it's okay if things don't go perfectly. Exploring professional guidance, like life coaching or therapy, can offer personalized strategies for maintaining balance. These professionals can provide tools and techniques tailored to your specific needs.

Plan your days blending moments of productivity with pockets of relaxation. You start with a morning walk, followed by a productive work session. Then, you take a break to enjoy a hobby like painting or gardening. In the afternoon, you catch up with a friend over coffee. By evening, you're winding down with a good book or favorite TV show. This balance creates a fulfilling, well-rounded lifestyle where you achieve your goals without sacrificing your peace of mind. It's about finding what works for you and embracing the joys of activity and rest.

8.6 Journaling and Reflective Writing

Reflective writing has a way of enhancing self-awareness and emotional well-being that's nothing short of magical. Reducing stress and anxiety through expressive writing is like having a conversation with your best friend, only this time, you're the listener, too.

Improving mood and emotional regulation is another perk. By jotting down your thoughts, you see patterns more quickly so you can better manage your emotions. Enhancing self-awareness and personal growth allows you to have insights about yourself. And let's remember the value of having a record of experiences and insights. It's like creating a personal time capsule that you can revisit whenever you need to remember how far you've come.

Starting a journaling practice doesn't require any fancy tools or profound revelations. Begin by choosing a comfortable time and place to write. Maybe it's first thing in the morning when the house is quiet or late at night when the world is asleep. Starting with simple prompts and free writing can help get the words flowing. Prompts like "What made me happy today?" or "What's one thing I'm grateful for?" are great starters.

You don't need to write a novel—just let your thoughts spill onto the page. Different journaling techniques can keep things interesting. Gratitude journals focus on positive thinking, helping you cultivate a habit of thankfulness. Bullet journals are perfect for those who love lists and organization, combining notes, to-do lists, and reflections in one place. Setting aside regular time for reflective writing makes it a habit. Be consistent with your journaling, whether it's a few minutes or half an hour.

Various types of journaling offer unique benefits, catering to different interests and goals. Gratitude journaling is fantastic for boosting your mood. By writing things you're thankful for daily, you start to have a positive outlook as your default. Reflective journaling is all about self-discovery. It's a space to explore your thoughts and emotions, helping you understand yourself better. Creative journaling with art and doodles can be incredibly freeing. Sometimes, words aren't enough, and that's where colors and shapes come in. Goal-setting and planning journals are excellent for those who like to stay organized. They help you keep track of your goals and the steps needed to achieve them, offering a sense of accomplishment.

Writer's block is a common hurdle, but prompts and guided journaling resources can help. Websites and books offer endless ideas to get you started. Encouraging short, regular writing sessions can overcome the barrier. Even five minutes a day can make a difference. Joining journaling groups or online communities provides support and accountability. Exploring digital journaling apps and tools can also make the process more convenient. Apps like **Day One** or **Penzu** offer features like prompts, reminders, and the ability to add photos, making journaling a more interactive experience.

To help with creating writing ideas, there are several great places to find writing prompts and ideas to spark creativity:

1. Online Prompt Generators

Reedsy: Offers a variety of writing prompts categorized by genre.

Writer's Digest: Provides weekly writing prompts.

Plot Generator: Automatically creates plot ideas, character names, and other story elements.

The Story Shack: Has a random prompt generator and character idea tools.

2. Books

642 Things to Write About: A popular book filled with interesting and unusual writing prompts.

The Writer's Idea Book **by Jack Heffron**: Combines prompts with exercises to help develop ideas.

3. Writing Communities

Reddit: Subreddits like r/WritingPrompts offer thousands of prompts shared by users.

Wattpad: Many writers share prompts and challenges on this platform.

Medium: Writers often publish lists of prompts or post ideas to inspire others.

4. Writing Courses and Workshops

Online courses like **MasterClass** and Coursera often include creative exercises and prompts.

Local writing workshops and groups sometimes provide shared writing challenges.

5. Creative Journals

Guided journals often include prompts to help develop thoughts and storylines. Examples include **"The 5-Minute Journal"** or other themed creativity journals.

6. Pinterest

Numerous boards are dedicated to writing prompts across all genres—fantasy, romance, thriller, etc.

7. News and Current Events

Reading headlines or articles can spark ideas for stories based on real-world events or social issues.

8. Everyday Observations

Draw inspiration from people-watching, personal experiences, and travels. Keep a notebook handy for random ideas that pop up throughout the day.

9. Writing Prompt Apps

Apps like **Writing Prompts by Writing.com** or **Prompts** offer daily writing ideas.

These resources can help jumpstart your creativity, whether you are looking for a new idea or trying to overcome writer's block!

Picture this: You've found your perfect journaling spot, armed with a favorite pen or a sleek digital app. Writing becomes a daily ritual, a moment of peace amid the chaos. Each entry helps you better understand yourself, manage stress, and appreciate the good in your life. You're not just recording events; you're capturing moments of growth and insight. This habit of reflective writing can transform your days and offer a sense of clarity and purpose that enriches your retirement years.

Bucket List Opportunities:

- Try Meditating

- Play Games and Work on Puzzles

- Review your Eating Habits

- Take a Nap

- Acknowledge Relaxation as Important

- Journal

Keeping the Adventure Alive

N ow that you have everything you need to start ticking off your retirement bucket list and living a fulfilling, exciting life, it's time to share your experience with others just beginning their journey.

By leaving your honest opinion of this book on Amazon, you'll help other retirees and soon-to-be retirees discover the tools, ideas, and inspiration they need to create the retirement they've always dreamed of. Your review doesn't just share your thoughts—it helps keep the spirit of retirement adventure alive for others looking for guidance and a roadmap for their golden years. I appreciate your help. The joy of retirement is kept alive when we share our stories, wisdom, and experiences—and you're helping us do just that.

https://www.amazon.com/review/create-review?&asin=B0DLYWC67K

Or scan the QR Code:

Conclusion

Conclusion

As we wrap up this transformative journey, we must recognize the diverse activities we've explored. From gardening clubs to geocaching, chair yoga, and lifelong learning, this book offers a wealth of options to help you create a life you love after retirement. Whether health-conscious, curious, or tech-savvy, there's something here for everyone. The key to a fulfilling, joyful retirement lies in staying active, discovering new passions, and maintaining social connections.

First, let's quickly stroll down memory lane and recap what we've covered. We started by building your social circle. During our conversation, we discussed how Frank transformed from a lonely retiree to a gardening enthusiast with an active social life. This transformation is about Frank and the sense of community and connection we can all build. We talked about joining local clubs, hosting gatherings, volunteering, and using social media to stay connected. We explored lifelong learning, encouraging you to explore new subjects and expand your horizons with online courses, local workshops, and educational travel.

We then moved on to physical wellness, highlighting gentle exercises like strength training, chair yoga, water aerobics, and Tai Chi. We also highlighted the significance of participating in walking clubs, hiking, and home-based fitness programs during our discussion. Creative hobbies and artistic pursuits came next, opening up a world of painting, knitting, photography, and more. We also discussed budget-friendly travel and local outings, visiting parks and museums, and attending community events without breaking the bank.

In the tech tips chapter, we walked through mastering smartphones, using social media, staying safe online, and making the most of video calls and health apps. We explored volunteering and giving back as an opportunity to share your wisdom and skills through mentoring, community arts programs, and environmental conservation. Finally, we delved into mind and body wellness, covering meditation, brain games, nutrition, sleep hygiene, and balancing relaxation and productivity.

Now, let's talk about some key takeaways. First, stay connected. Loneliness is a sneaky little beast, but you can fight it by building a solid social circle. Join clubs, attend events, and don't be afraid to reach out to new people. Second, never stop learning. Keeping your brain active is fundamental to aging well, whether it's a new language, a DIY craft, or an online course. Third, take care of your body. The building blocks of a healthy, happy life are gentle exercises, balanced nutrition, and good sleep hygiene. Fourth, embrace creativity. Artistic pursuits like painting, knitting, and photography can bring immense joy and satisfaction. Fifth, give back. Volunteering helps others and gives you a sense of purpose and fulfillment.

So, what's next? It's time to take the first steps towards your enhanced retirement and dream trip. Whether it's joining a local club, signing up for an online course, starting a new exercise routine, or picking up a paintbrush for the first time, the key is to take that first step today. Don't wait for the 'perfect' moment because it might never come. Life is happening right now, so dive in and make the most of it.

Remember, retirement is not the end; it's a new beginning. It's your time to explore, discover, and enjoy. You've got a wealth of experience and wisdom, and now you have the time to share it and use it to enrich your life and the lives of others. Try new things, meet new people, and embrace the adventure.

I'm cheering you on every step of the way. You've got this! Whether planting a garden, learning a new skill, or volunteering at a local shelter, know that you are making a difference. Your retirement years can be some of your life's most rewarding and fulfilling. So, here's to your new chapter, filled with joy, adventure, and endless possibilities. Happy retirement!

	TO DO:
☑	find your passion
☑	try something new
☑	enjoy life!

Special Section–
Planning Your Dream
Trip!

Here's a detailed outline to help you plan your dream trip, an adventure waiting to unfold:

1. Define Your Vision

- **Destination**: Where do you want to go? Explore multiple destinations if undecided.

- **Type of Trip**: Adventure, relaxation, cultural exploration, nature, etc.

- **Length of Stay**: How many days or weeks? Consider travel time.

- **Travel Companions**: Are you traveling solo, with family, or with friends?

2. Set a Budget

- **Total Budget**: Determine your overall spending limit.

- **Breakdown**:

  - Flights/Transportation

  - Accommodation

  - Daily expenses (food, activities, souvenirs)

  - Emergency fund

- **Savings Plan**: How will you save? Set a realistic timeline for saving.

3. Research Destinations

- **Weather & Best Travel Times**: Consider peak season vs. off-season for affordability.

- **Must-See Attractions**: List your top places to visit.

- **Cultural Highlights**: Research local festivals, cultural practices, and language.

4. Plan the Logistics

- **Transportation**:

- Book flights, trains, or car rentals.

- Research public transportation options.

- **Accommodations**:

  - Choose hotels, hostels, vacation rentals, or unique stays (e.g., glamping, cabins).

  - Book early to secure the best rates.

- **Travel Insurance**: Purchase coverage for health, cancelations, and lost items.

5. Craft Your Itinerary

- **Day-by-Day Schedule**:

  - Include must-see attractions, tours, and activities.

  - Balance active days with downtime.

- **Special Experiences**: Book unique activities like cooking classes, guided tours, or adventure excursions.

- **Dining Options**: Research local restaurants, street food, and culinary experiences.

6. Health and Safety

- **Vaccinations and Medications**: Check if any are required for your destination.

- **Travel Advisories**: Research any safety alerts or precautions.

- **Local Emergency Contacts**: Know the numbers for medical help and your country's embassy.

7. Pack Strategically

- **Essential Items**:

  - Travel documents (passport, visas, insurance).

  - Clothing for the climate and activities.

  - Toiletries, medications, and tech essentials (chargers, adapters).

- **Travel Gear**: Backpacks, suitcases, travel locks, and comfortable shoes.

- **Travel Apps**: Download maps, translation apps, and itinerary organizers.

8. Prepare for Departure

- **Documents**: Ensure all travel documents are up-to-date and printed.

- **Home Arrangements**: Arrange pet care, mail forwarding, and house-sitting.

- **Currency**: Exchange money or notify your bank about international transactions.

- **Confirm Reservations**: Double-check all bookings (flights, accommodations, tours).

9. Enjoy the Journey

- **Stay Flexible**: Leave room for spontaneity and last-minute changes.

- **Document the Experience**: Take photos, journal, or blog about your travels.

- **Connect with Locals**: Engage with people to make your experience richer.

10. Post-Trip Reflection

- **Evaluate**: What worked well, and what would you change next time?

- **Share**: Create a memory book, share photos, or write about your trip.

- **Plan the Next Trip**: Start thinking about your next dream destination!

This outline should give you a solid foundation to plan your dream trip, balancing preparation with excitement.

References

Made in United States
Cleveland, OH
19 March 2025

15324689R00083